What Others Are Saying...

Too few followers of Jesus understand the church calendar. In this helpful book, Schwarzentraub not only walks you through the themes of the season, but helps you practice rhythms to aid you in the strengthening of your Christian faith. Read it and live life with a fresh sense of purpose.

—GARY HOAG, SPIRITUAL COUNSEL, GENEROSITY MONK

A deeply spiritual guide to help us appreciate the various seasons and emotions reflected throughout the year.... I'd like to incorporate some ideas of hope and renewal into my own spiritual life in the coming seasons of this, and every year.

—REV. BONNIE MCGRAW

Some great ideas in the "Things to Do" sections. If your worship team is looking for a resource, this is the book that I would suggest.

—KANDI WEIDER, CALIFORNIA-NEVADA CERTIFIED LAY MINISTRY COMMITTEE MEMBER AND DISTRICT LAY LEADER

For parents, this is a wonderful book for teaching children in a relatable way with some fun teaching projects....

—ROGER PECK, WEBSITE DEVELOPER FOR NONPROFIT WEBSITES

We see, feel, smell, taste and hear things that we are to experience each part of the Liturgical Year.

—CAROL S. KERN, CHURCH MUSICIAN AND VISUAL ARTIST

Presents a way to restore balance by living the year with biblical celebrations and holidays in your own home....

—P. L. CLARK, AUTHOR

Offers comfort, hope and encouragement for the potential disorientation [and] uncertainty [in these]current times....
—Barbara Young, RN, author of *The Heart That Rocks Health Care* and Conscious Living educator

What a refreshing way of bringing the Christian view into perspective.... Brings Peter's story alive.... This book is practical, well-organized, and easy to read.
—Mary Mohs, spiritual director and author

Specifically addresses using Christian principles to deal with the aftermath of Covid, but provides help with all the issues that affect us today. Highly recommended....
—George Hahn, author

Provides a remedy in setting out the rhythms of the seasons as gifts from a loving and generous God....
—June Gillam, novelist, poet and church librarian

Themes of thankfulness and trusting in Jesus abound...A different approach toward dealing with loss in the present pandemic world or at any time we feel ourselves encumbered with difficult circumstances that threaten our relationship with God.... Encouraging and meaningful on many levels....
—Kelly Lardner, author

If you have wanted to learn more about the Christian seasons in an approachable way, this is a great book to do so. I most appreciated the practicality and easy to understand nature of how the topic was addressed.
—Rev. Dave Pettengill

I especially like Betsy's take on Peter on the water. What a clever insight and delivery. Informative for liturgical seasons of the year and an easy and enjoyable read.

—KATHY O'DELL, CERTIFIED LAY SERVANT AND CHURCH LAY LEADER

I appreciated the deep thought that went into the book [and] learning more about the Sabbath versus Sunday....A great overview of the liturgical year for laity and clergy. I recommend it for all church and worship leaders.

—REV. MATT PEARSON

I loved loved loved this book. I am reading it for a second time. The story of Peter I loved. I like having a simple reference to go to.

—ROBIN SHANDA, CERTIFIED LAY SERVANT

The book opens another way for me to get to know God and worship Him.

—REV. CHRIS MCANALLY

.

Tossed in TIME

STEERING BY THE CHRISTIAN SEASONS

Betsy Schwarzentraub

For related resources, see www.generousstewards.com.

ISBN 978-1-5323-8870-5
Library of Congress Control Number: 2021914797

Generous Stewards Communications
Elk Grove, CA 95624

Text design and composition by John Reinhardt Book Design

Printed in the United States of America

Dedicated to Ken, my soulmate

Contents

ONE

After the Storm

EVERYONE AROUND GALILEE knows me as Simon the fisherman —But the Teacher gave me another name: Peter, the Rock.

Ha! I suppose I am substantial enough at times, maybe even stubborn enough, to be a leader for the guys—a small band of believers who follow the Teacher around while he brings the Word. There's no doubt I've had my moments, when I let my passion get the best of me.

All the same, my exuberance sometimes leads to incredible experiences—like the time I jumped out of a perfectly good boat into a raging sea!

It started when the Teacher was winding up a day-long marathon of teaching. He'd drawn a good crowd to that grassy meadow — you know the one—beside the Sea of Galilee. And he kept them there with story after story. Whether they got the message or not, they loved listening to him. He thanked them all with the miracle of the loaves and fishes: Everybody's heard about it, but you had to be there to see it for yourself. Heaps of barley loaves, masses of fresh fish where there had been only trampled grass a moment before. The people went nuts. Amid the feasting, a few even remembered to thank him.

It had been quite a day. We were spent. The Teacher sent us on ahead to Bethsaida in one of the bigger fishing boats. It was able to hold all of us. He said he would follow shortly. No doubt one of the other fishermen could bring him along. But people always wanted to hear more. There was no telling when he would be able to break away.

On the other hand, he might decide to stay back for a while to catch his breath from all that teaching and healing.

We knew how much he cherished his quiet time for prayer. So we set out, hoisting the sail to a gentle breeze. The Teacher, the people and the meadow got smaller and smaller, and the shadows began to lengthen.

Far below sea level, the Galilee is a fresh water lake, but we call it a "sea." That's because it›s so wide no one can see from one side to the other, and nobody's ever found the bottom. Most of the time it's as meek as a lamb. But other times the wind comes down off the surrounding mountains and stirs the water up into a terrible fury. Then the lamb turns into a heaving, raging monster in the blink of an eye. When that happens, even the most seasoned fishermen head for shore.

That's what happened to us that day: everything going along smooth as you please, the sail drawing nicely, Andrew keeping an eye out astern for the Teacher in a following boat. And then WOOOSH! The wind came down, the waves kicked up. And we were scrambling for dear life. Worse! Night was coming on.

James and John struggled to haul down the thrashing sail, Andrew and I bailed frantically, even as the towering waves dumped more water aboard. We were all soaked through in a moment. The landlubbers among us cowered in the bottom, bemoaning their fate. The boat tossed about dangerously.

Now it was truly dark, and still the Teacher hadn't shown up. How could he dare set out in such terrible weather? Maybe the Teacher had seen it coming and had stayed behind. Either way, we all had more than we could handle with this full-on gale, just trying to keep upright in those crosscurrents and waves. The wind pitched up even more. I could only hope he would safely wait out the storm. On the other hand, our own chances in this little chip of a vessel became dimmer by the minute.

We could see nothing until it hit us. Through the howling night we bailed like madmen, each taking up the pail when the other gave out. Andrew stopped watching for the Teacher: we had to see to our own survival. We stuffed rags in the leaks to little effect. We clung on with white knuckles. I knew the Teacher—even if he were unwise enough to embark— would never find us in this turmoil.

At the darkest hour, our labors faltered; we were exhausted. Matthew peered out into the night and shouted in fear. "Look!"

Everyone aboard followed his pointing finger. We glimpsed through the heaving water and flying spray a mere smudge of light, distant, indistinct, a scrap of fog, perhaps. Why was it not shredded in an instant? No, a pillar of wavering light, most certainly, moved unerringly toward us. We watched it approach, transfixed by fear.

Now it seemed to be a figure. "t's a ghost!" cried Nathaniel. "We're doomed!"

We were grown men; we'd seen a lot over the years. But I'm not too proud to admit we were terrified.

Closer, the light took on form. Just as we could make out a face, his voice came to us, despite the roar of the tempest. "Take heart. It is I. Don't be afraid."

And there was the Teacher's catchphrase: "Don't be afraid." He was always saying that. Probably because we always needed to hear it. My heart leapt into my throat. It was our Teacher! But how could this be? I looked for a deck beneath his feet. No deck. Nor did he grasp at anything to steady himself. No boat! He was utterly alone, striding on the water. Where he stepped the waves subsided as if into a garden path.

His words were the final affirmation. He said, "It is I." That's something nobody says, because in Hebrew it's so close to the Divine Name for the Giver of Life. The Holy One gave that name to our ancestor Moses generations ago at the burning bush. Nobody uses any word with that verb form in our language, because God is...well, God.

Except the Teacher. He is the only one who dares use a phrase so intimately related to the Almighty. (No wonder the religious authorities wanted him done away with.) So it had to be Jesus, the man I know and trust with my life. Here he was doing the impossible, as he was known to do. Not only did he brave the storm to seek us out, he didn't wait for a boat, but stepped directly on his way, and the treacherous maelstrom lay down like a kitten at his approach.

Well, if he could have that kind of courage to be out walking on top of the waves and saying the Name of the Holy One—then I could have courage, too.

I raised up and called to him. "Teacher, if it's really you, invite me to come out and join you." My impetuousness again. He clearly had mastery of the natural elements, not merely our sorry human souls.

My shipmates turned to me, aghast. My brother shouted, "Simon, no!"

I ignored them. I thought Jesus was going to break into a laugh, but he simply said, "Come."

So I did.

I clambered out of the pitching craft. My companions wailed horror and despair. I just kept my eyes right on Jesus. I put my feet on the water and stood. My fingers at last released the gunnel, and I stepped forward. I took a second step. Jesus smiled gentle encouragement as he stepped across the water toward me.

Exhilaration seized me. I was doing it! After all, either you trust him, or you don't. I was walking on water to Jesus! I beamed my triumph at him. What a story to tell! I was only dimly aware of the tempest that raged outside our bond.

But everyone has limits. Mine came quickly. With all that howling of the wind around me and the chaos below, I couldn't resist taking a peek at my feet. That was the crazy thing—taking my eyes off Jesus once I was out there.

I glanced down at the bottomless liquid below my feet. Fear struck my sailor's heart. Before I could gasp, I was in the drink! I came up sputtering, flailing. Under again. "Master, save me!" Did I shout it or only wish it? He reached down and pulled me up.

He held me over the water while I dripped with shame. In the faint predawn light his face flickered between compassion and amusement. He asked with a note of sadness, "Why did you doubt?"

I know I'm a grown man, but I just wanted to die, or to curl up in his lap and sob out my remorse. The thing is, either you trust him, or you don't. That's what faith is, after all.

I squeezed my eyes shut so I wouldn't see his sympathy. When I opened them again, we were both in the boat. All around us the storm had quit, just like that. The waves subsided to the merest ripple, the screaming gale dwindled to barely a breeze.

As one, all of us flopped down on the floorboards at the Teacher's feet and worshipped him. "You are not only the Teacher," we cried. "You've got to be the Son of God!"

—Based on Matthew 14:22–33

TWO

Lost at Sea

————◄○►————

PETER REFLECTS ON THE STORM:

IT TAKES A LOT FOR ME to admit it, but even I was afraid out in the storm that night. After all, I'm Simon, the big, brash fisherman who's first to get into a fight and the last to back down. But that was more than any squall I'd ever seen.

Yes, four of us were commercial fishermen. We'd experienced sudden storms sweeping over Galilee, but usually it was from the safety of shore. All the same, that wind was far worse than just any squall. In the middle of the night, no less. What would become of us?

I know every day we live is a gift from our Creator. But when a frightening time comes, when everything we've been comfortable with has been thrown overboard, it's easy to lose our way and forget what gives us a sense of what's normal. When I hurt or I've lost people I care about, it feels like a great stone weight.

————◄○►————

NO DOUBT PETER and the rest of the disciples could taste their fear that night, in their fragile boat in the windstorm on the Sea of Galilee. Yes, four of the twelve disciples ("the guys," as Peter might have called them), were fishermen by trade. They had been out on the lake all their lives. But they were all past the point of exhaustion, battling the wind and waves in the deepest part of the night. As if that wasn't bad enough, they were certain they saw a ghost out there stalking them on the wild waves! It's a wonder they didn't give up altogether.

So what about a virus that suddenly sweeps in like a storm and swirls all around the globe? As of August 2, 2023, the World Health Organization reported 768,983,095 confirmed cases of COVID-19 worldwide, including 6,953,743 deaths. Of these, the United States of America had 103,436,829 people struck by the illness and 1,127,152 deaths.

But that's not all. How do we count the millions more people who have lost their jobs, businesses, savings, or homes in the wake of the downturned economy? With grim reports assailing us even now, we may be able to taste our own fears. We may feel unsure about keeping our personal boat afloat—for long-term health, livelihood, or relationships with people whose views of the pandemic and its fallout differ from our own.

While many parts of the world have countered deadly blows from the initial pandemic, people in more economically privileged countries can fitfully emerge from the pandemic lockdown. But as each society has reopened, many individuals continue to see themselves alone, as if piloting their own little vessels through the uncertain waters.

Living beyond the first waves of the COVID-19 pandemic, we may still feel as if a multi-dimensional storm rushed down on us. Just grappling with a single dimension of it—the sense of meaningful movement through time—can be overwhelming. Time itself is a gift from God, but we can experience it like an adverse wind pushing against us. It may throw us into wild waves in a desperate search to keep busy, or else into a deadly stillness that isolates us in emotional doldrums. So many in-person group activities have remained suspended or have simply quit since the pandemic attack. Thousands are still

unable or afraid to go to work, stores, restaurants, movies, or gatherings with friends. They have lost their social bearings.

If we have children or grandchildren, we may have decided to keep home-schooling them while working fulltime at home, as well. Millions of people have lost their jobs, and millions more left their work to look for something better.

Even when we decide to get together now for birthdays or holidays, those don't seem like the old, cherished traditions. And a myriad small social interactions that used to provide a sense of community may still make us feel vulnerable: physical activities, events with friends, attending community events, visits to the library.

Just as important, our time milestones for the year have disappeared or feel downright dangerous. How do we navigate activities and decide what is low risk and what is high? Stories abound about people who abandoned caution, went to crowded events, and then caught the deadly disease. What is worth the risk of another virus variation?

For those who try to follow Jesus, worst of all can be the loss of in-person, weekly worship. Regularly gathering in faith with even a few other people can remind us of God, who is the Master of all, including life's wild storms. Whether we used to go to church every Sunday or we didn't attend all that often, we knew it was there. Church may have given us a sense of safe haven when we were buffeted by life's storms. Now, at different stages of dealing with a pernicious global virus and its uncertain aftermath, how can we re-shape our sense of time when so many social markers have been lost in the tumult?

Tossed about in this way, we may find the word "tumult" aptly describes what we are going through. The term can mean havoc in at least three ways. First, it could be an uproar: a violent commotion or disturbance. Second, it might be a general outbreak or uprising. A silent but deadly virus can create such an upheaval externally, with citizens scrambling for medical care or protesting government edicts. Third, it may describe a highly distressed mind or set of emotions. This definition got me thinking. Those years of the COVID-19 pandemic have created a disturbance in everyone's life. Its effects have caused an external upheaval, with citizens scrambling for medical care or protesting government edicts. And the silent but deadly virus has preyed on millions of people's lives, minds, and emotions. The resulting unrest and turbulence has entire sectors of society struggling to get their bearings once more. In all these understandings of the word, our sense of meaningful time has been tossed overboard.

Alternatively, getting caught "adrift" on the open sea can be just as deadly as the stirred-up gale itself. A boat adrift with no horizon in sight can mean slow death for the people aboard, if they're unable to steer by the stars or to communicate with other vessels to get back to land. Likewise, those who remain can get caught in eddies of grief after the loss of those they cared for. Or they may get locked into more complicated laments when the ones they have lost had refused the vaccine.

At the same time, even if (on the surface) life seems smooth, what might be moving through the watery depths below us can be even more lethal than the original storm. Most people now know that a virus can mutate and attack us unawares. Survivors of a first virus surge may fear continued vulnerability to a more resistant variant. Or people may become so accustomed to isolation or so steeped in distrust of others that they lose their sense of human community. In addition, they might lose their faith in God. Or their trust of other people. Or their sense of purposeful movement through specific times in their lives.

Granted, history gives us hope for the big picture, since humanity has experienced more than one plague or pandemic, and some people have survived. The bubonic plague, known as the "Black Death," occurred in Western Eurasia and North Africa from 1346 to 1353, causing the deaths of 75 to 200 million people. That was from 30 to 50 percent of the entire population of Europe at that time. The pandemic eased with better sanitation, hygiene, and medical advancements, but never completely disappeared. Its eventual weakening was likely due to the practice of quarantining infected people. These days, it can be treated and cured with antibiotics.

Then there was the Great Plague of 1665, the worst outbreak of plague in England since 1348. London lost roughly 15% of its population, and the virus spread to other parts of that country. Researchers say the virus abated as people started to develop a stronger immunity to the disease, and as more effective quarantine methods were used for ships coming into the country.

Another example is the Great Influenza Epidemic, misnamed the "Spanish Flu," which hit in 1916. About 500 million people fell prey to it, and at least 50 million of them died, 675,000 of them in the United States. In the year 1918, it produced more casualties than World War I, World War II, the Korean War, and the Vietnam War combined. Scientists say that eventually people either had prior exposure to the virus or it became less life threatening. Scientists worked feverishly on finding a vaccine, but before they could develop it, the virus disappeared.

So there is hope. People are still here on this Earth. In most places around the globe, we have benefitted from better hygiene, medical advancements, antibiotics, vaccines, more effective quarantines, and an eventual lessening of the virus itself.

But knowing history and our "eventual" survival as people doesn't guarantee a current feeling of assurance. There are other factors these days on the stormy seas. Some feel uncertain about valuing community altogether, even wondering whether or not they *want* to return to their former human connections. After health and safety issues required a lockdown for months on end, rafts of people intensified their habits of working at home and "cocooning" there for entertainment as well.

The repercussions of the pandemic isolation have hit children and youth especially hard. Not only have countless students lost the effectiveness of in-person learning, many have developed a lifestyle that is more comfortable with electronics than with personal interaction. Near-constant communication may take place, but without face-to-face relationship. It's not surprising that cyber-bullying has increased in recent years.

Teen suicides have become a cause for alarm. A study under the National Institutes of Health identified 5,568 youth from 5 to 24 years old who died by suicide during the first ten months of the pandemic—a number was higher than the expected number of deaths had there been no virus spread. The number of deaths by suicide were higher than expected among males, preteens from 5 to12 years old, young adults aged 18 to 24 years, non-Hispanic American Indians or Alaskan Native youth, and non-Hispanic Black youth, in contrast to before the pandemic. Suicide deaths involving firearms were also higher than expected.

But that study was just for the first ten months. "This research is only a first step in examining the pandemic's impact on youth mental health," the report said. Clearly it "does not reflect longer-term trends in youth suicide that may have changed as the pandemic wore on." There is much more to be done to realize the long-term cost among American children and youth.

Beyond those concerns, extreme weather events add to this perfect storm for humanity. Scientists are finding a stronger link than previously realized between the planet's warming and more dangerous worldwide weather patterns. Around the globe, people are experiencing bigger storm surges, greater snowfall, hotter heat waves, and more pervasive droughts. "The era of global warming is over; 'now we're in the age of 'global boiling,'" an article said in the August 11, 2023 issue of *The Week* magazine. Based on several sources, it noted that July, 2023 was likely the world's hottest month on record, water temperatures hit 101 degrees in the ocean off Florida, and basic rhythms of human behavior are being reordered as the mercury rises. [1] These phenomena cannot help but lead to a greater sense of human vulnerability in the face of nature gone wild.

One more factor augments the storm around us: easy access to images of societal disruption and arbitrary violence. Yes, "wars and rumors of wars" have occurred for uncounted centuries. But now a soldier's pictures of the resulting devastation comes into our living rooms and onto our electronic devices on a daily basis. It's as if we personally witness the mass shootings and attempts at violent revolt all around the globe.

The impact of social media takes this disruption further. Social media Chief Executive Officers themselves have admitted an unforeseen effect of their software: more and more extreme perspectives.[2] Their media algorithms are set to follow the users' individual preferences, automatically feeding more articles solely from that the viewer's perspective. The result is a widening gap within the general population of what are the "basic facts," and accusations that other viewpoints are "false news."

In stark contrast to all that bad news, *Tossed in Time* announces the *Good* News. As a message from an old hymn, *Stand By Me,* reminds us, "when the storms of life are raging," Jesus Christ always stands with us. Casting about for a meaningful guide in all the confusion, we can look to a different way of counting our days. The Christian Calendar offers a foundational rhythm that holds our lives together. It has worship seasons that are so ancient, they are new to almost all of us. So keeping our sights on these seasons can offer personal bearings even when we feel as if we are far out on the unpredictable sea.

Talking About God

Talking about God is always a tricky business. The One we call Love, the Mystery beneath all of life, goes far beyond any words human beings could utter. But still we try to express something of God's fullness as we glimpse it in our lives. The different phrases for "God" in this book are meant to prompt you into thinking about your own experiences and the ways people have spoken about God in different cultures and times.

For roughly forty years or so, I honored God by saying aloud the personal name God gave to Moses at the burning bush (Exodus 3:14). Those four letters, YHWH, are not spoken by Jews, our current siblings in faith and the people of our Christian Old Testament. They do this as a way of honoring God, and use a substitute phrase meaning "I Am Who I Am." English language Bibles usually substitute the word "the LORD." After prayer and conversation with Jewish and Christian colleagues, I decided to *not* say God's sacred name as a way of honoring our Loving Parent, the One whom Jesus called *Abba*, which means "Daddy." So I use other phrases instead. There are plenty of names for God in the Bible and in Christian literature. I have used some of them throughout this text, and I invite you to use the name that is most meaningful to you.

A Note on the Illustrations

The line drawings in this expanded edition reflect my conviction that Jesus Christ is as alive now as he was with the first disciples centuries ago. The pictures can remind us that he is active among us, especially in times of transition or uncertainty. Drawings throughout this text show Jesus with people in various settings, and particularly with children. Children often go unnoticed, despite God's call to care for those who are seen as "the least of these" among us. These scenes also can remind us that God considers every one of us as God's child, regardless of our age or situation.

These illustrations match the mood of each chapter, such as exhaustion when we feel lost at sea, recognizing broken relationships during Lent, and joyful anticipation of Christ's coming in Advent. I invite you to enjoy them as they tell a story of their own.

How to Use This Book

As a reader, you can use **Tossed in Time** in different ways, depending on your circumstances. You've already read "After the Storm." Now you could:

- Read through this book from its beginning, no matter what time of year you pick up the book. Take as much time as you want to explore the ideas, questions, and activities to bring the meaning of the season into your home and life. You might also feel led to journal, or to send a note to someone who comes to mind related to one of the chapter themes.
- Go by the month of the year you are in—Note the time of year in the Table of Contents. See if there are special days or themes within that period that take on a different or deeper meaning for you. Consider doing an activity that might become a habit or ritual to help you remember what's important about this time.
- Start at the beginning of either three-season cycle, with either Advent or Lent. Consider how your faith or understanding can develop from Advent to Christmas to Epiphany, or from Lent to Easter to Pentecost. Bible passages are listed just for those who want to follow up on a thought, not for argument or "proof." Don't let religious terms get in the way. Notice your own emotions that are

revealed in each part of the cycle. Think how the themes may give a sense of connection to this time in your life.

- However you choose to use this book, I hope it offers you some essential bearings in the midst of what otherwise could be a time of uncertainty, fear, or loss. May you rediscover Jesus Christ as someone to trust, establish some seasonal markers as you go along, and find ways to celebrate these occasions as you dare to experience the time of your life.

Betsy Schwarzentraub

Finding Our Bearings

The Christian Year

ALL YEAR LONG

PETER REFLECTS ON THE STORM:

MOST EVERYONE has to deal with chaos at some time in their lives. It's easy to lose our bearings in the middle of it. If I'm out fishing and it's a clear night, I can steer by the stars. But there are plenty of times when storm clouds conceal them. And life onshore can be even harder to navigate sometimes.

When I have the courage to look for Jesus somewhere out in the middle of the trouble, it helps. My life may seem to go down the drain in lots of ways, but if I look straight at what's going on, I might see what the God of Israel is doing in the middle of the tumult. So is there any framework that can help me be at home with God, even in the midst of all that commotion?

WHAT IF THERE WERE a different kind of calendar to mark our days, to help us remember what's really important?

I grew up assuming that everyone goes by one calendar. The year begins in January and ends in December. It never occurred to me that a calendar could be anything different. As an adult, I saw that Jewish months have different names and start at different times. I also felt the Jewish calendar was full of spiritually significant days. Later, when our family expanded, I learned that Muslims use different months and have other names, also based in religion. Then I discovered that a lot of the names for months and days in my familiar calendar, like January and Sunday, come from names the ancient Romans gave to their gods!

So what is the Christian calendar?

THEME 1: A Different Calendar

The calendar used in parts of the world influenced by a European heritage comes from a kaleidoscope of viewpoints and traditions. The Christmas cycle, for example, starting with Advent and going through Epiphany (November through February) is based on the non-Jewish ("Gentile") calendar. Wherever the ancient Romans went, they brought their way of keeping time with them. Key dates in that calendar stay the same from year to year, such as December 25 for Christmas Day. But the Easter cycle, starting with Lent and going through Pentecost (late March or April through early November) is based on the Jewish calendar and follows the movements of the moon.

Together, these two cycles give Jesus followers a primary rhythm year after year, regardless of social holidays and other celebrations in the wider community. Both cycles are bracketed by hope. In the first cycle, Advent is on the front end, with hope in the birth of Jesus Christ on Earth. On the back end of that cycle is Epiphany: hope in the Good News

of God's love going out to all the world. Then in the second cycle, on the front end there's Lent: the promise of new beginnings through divine forgiveness. And on the back end is Pentecost: hope in Christ's final coming at the end of time. It's not that we need to go around living day to day with the end times in our mind. But for those who choose to notice the worship seasons, there is both unity and balance.

For several years, I trained people to become volunteer pastors of congregations. A portion of that teaching dealt with the Christian Year. One of the most creative and exciting things I've done to teach the Christian Year was with worship leader Carol Kern, who is an extraordinary church musician and visual artist.

The project involved refrigerator boxes.

It offered participants a walk-through experience. Carol went to appliance stores and picked up the huge cardboard containers in which the stores received refrigerators. That was a win-win, since they were going to throw out the boxes anyway. When standing up, the containers were at least five and a half feet tall.

We left one side of each box open and then painted both the insides and the outsides of the boxes with the season's color: purple for Advent and Lent, white for Christmas and Easter, green for Epiphany, and red for the day of Pentecost and green for the ordered days that follow it. Then we added seasonal sayings and borrowed worship banners from churches to drape over the top of the open box panels. Finally, we made or found various symbols related to each season, using the five senses. A circle of candles surrounded the Christ candle for Advent, recorded Christmas carols allowed visitors to sing along at Christmas, fragrant frankincense recalled the coming of the wise men in Epiphany, and so on. Every person had a handout sheet with things they could do at each station, including questions to ponder.

THEME 2: Two Cycles

I first saw a colored chart of the worship seasons long before doing the workshop with Carol. It was composed of two half-circles of color, divided horizontally, with each half moving from purple on the left, through white in the center, to green on the right. The first color was purple for Advent, next white for Christmas, then green for Epiphany. Beneath that half-circle came purple for Lent, white for Easter, then a sliver of red for Pentecost Day and green for the rest of the Pentecost season.

Seeing the year this way, the two purple seasons of Advent and Lent are times to *prepare* by turning our lives back toward God. During Advent, the four weeks before Christmas Day, we can slow down to reflect on our lives, admit our brokenness and need for healing, and actively wait for the One who seeks to come more deeply into our lives. Then in the second half of the year, Lent does the same thing before Easter. If we're struggling with our own failings, feeling vulnerable and broken, or mourning those we have lost, the worship seasons remind us of the One who ultimately overcomes all suffering and separation.

The white periods of Christmas and Easter in the second stage give us cause to **celebrate**. Multiple days of Christmas remind us that the Creator of the cosmos comes alongside us, into every part of human life. The Easter season reveals Jesus' victory over death on our behalf, offering a radiant way of living both now and beyond death. Both seasons give us many days to praise God's goodness and claim our joy.

Then in the third, green stage of Epiphany and Pentecost, we **respond** with "So what do I do now?" Do I dare to live, not with easy answers, but with a fuller trust in God? Is there a way I can conduct my daily life that better expresses the Good News of forgiveness and new beginnings? How can I help change the destructive systems in which we live, or at least help heal the hurt that they cause?

Technically, this green stage includes what church scholars call "Ordinary Time," but the word "ordinary" can be misleading. It does *not* mean ho-hum, run-of-the-mill days. The term is related to the word "ordinal," meaning "coming in order." Ordinary time is when many of our common Scripture readings present some Books of the Bible from the beginning to end over successive weeks, to share the unique message of that particular biblical writer. For most Christians around the globe, it is clearer and simpler to identify those "ordered" days with the seasons of Epiphany and Pentecost to which they relate. That is what I chose to do in this book, as well.

Now the worship year is portrayed as one big circle instead of two halves. Currently there are about 2.3 billion Christians worldwide. Two billion of them are part of the "Western Church." It includes most of the Catholic Church, Western Protestant denominations around the globe, and their offshoots. For these Christians, the circle of the Christian Year begins in Advent and comes all the way around to Pentecost, which leads into Advent once again.

There are many reasons to imagine the year as a circle. Throughout human history, the circle has been a universal symbol, most often representing wholeness, original perfection, timelessness, and cycles of movement. In Chinese culture, the Tai Chi circle stands for harmony, balancing yin and yang: the mixture of two energies that make life possible. People have also seen the circle as a symbol for God, who is at the center of everything and has no circumference. For Native Americans, the traditional sacred circle stands for the four seasons, the universe, and the cycle of life.

So how does the full circle work for the Christian Year? As author K.C. Ireton says, its cyclical nature gives us "repeated opportunities to live out various aspects of our faith, to see life through the lens of the Christ-story and to deepen our understanding of what it means to be a follower of Jesus."[1]

So we recall the circle of the seasons as it moves through two cycles:

1. **Advent:** preparing for Christ's coming more deeply into our lives—**Christmas:** celebrating Jesus as *Emmanuel*, God With Us—**Epiphany**: seeing the Light of Christ in the world.

2. **Lent:** taking stock of our lives and getting back on track—**Easter**: the mystery of Christ, who has defeated death—**Pentecost**: living with God's Spirit active in our lives.

THEME 3: The Difference the Christian Year Can Make

Time makes a big difference for an anchored life. For example, Dietrich Bonhoeffer (1906 – 1945) was a pastor, professor, theologian, anti-Nazi activist, and key founding member of the "Confessing Church" that opposed the Nazi regime. He was clear about the distinction between personal faith and institutional religion and had seen the complete failure of the German Protestant church in the face of fascism.

Bonhoeffer was arrested by the Gestapo in 1943 and thrown in prison. Accused of participation in an exposed plot to kill Hitler, he was eventually taken to Flossenburg concentration camp. There he was hanged just two weeks before U.S. soldiers liberated that place of suffering and death.

All the time he was in prison, Bonhoeffer wrote letters, sermons, and Christian papers, which his family and sympathetic guards passed on to the outside world. His *Letters and Papers from Prison* includes more than two hundred writings.

Locked away from every social connection he had ever known, Bonhoeffer could tell time only by remembering the Christian worship-seasons and special days throughout the year. That was how he marked time: remembering parts of hymns and memorized prayers, encouraging or worshiping with other prisoners when allowed some moments together, and praying for people and circumstances in the wider world. In that way he kept tethered to the continuity of worship and prayer under the defining story of Christ.

By keeping his worship bearings, Bonhoeffer was able to know where he was in that Nazi storm. As a result, his life and writings continue to exert a huge influence on Christians across broad denominations and ideologies, from religious conservatives to non-affiliated liberals, from the Civil Rights movement in the United States to the anti-Apartheid movement in South Africa and anti-communist movements in

Eastern Europe. His enforced "sheltering in place" did not keep him from his purpose and from meaningful living.

QUESTIONS:

1. What days do I want or need to remember as I look forward to the year ahead? What would I like to research in order to celebrate those dates in a more significant way? Are there other people I would like to include in those remembrances or celebrations?
2. What would help me be more mindful of the worship rhythms of my life? Where in my home could I put something to represent each worship season as it arrives?
3. How could I prepare for Christmas and for Easter in a more thoughtful way? How might that different kind of preparation affect the way I, or we, mark those events at home?

THINGS TO DO:

1. Set up a candle on your dinner table to repeat a phrase each season. For example, today you might say:

   CANDLELIGHTER: "Giver of both time and eternity,"
   ALL AT THE TABLE: "my life is in your loving hands."

2. Write down the essential dates you want to remember this year. What birthdays or anniversaries? What natural seasons? Look at the first page of each of the chapters on the seasons in this book, then put the first day of each worship season in your calendar. As you read about that time in this book, consider one thing you

might like to do to pay more attention to its themes in your life.

3. Read Matthew 14:22–33 for yourself. Imagine what it must have been like that day at the feeding of the five thousand, then when Jesus' followers were sent off in the boat, and finally through that long, fearful night. What stands out the most about those events? What would all of that have been like for you? Start a personal journal or try a poem or a picture showing one of those scenes.

4. Create your own smaller version of the seasonal refrigerator boxes by using a file folder for each worship season. When decorated, it can stand on a table in your home. Use water-based paint to do the background color, then make or find symbols of the season that invite engagement. Cut out pictures from magazines or elsewhere that reflect the themes of the season. They are listed as themes in each chapter of this book and also on the worship cycle charts of the "Worship Arts" workshop in the appendix.

Let family members help you put the stand-up folder together. Have a Bible there to read any related verses. Talk with one another about the significance of the season. Take a picture of your creation, so you can remember the experience and do something different with that same season the following year.

Arthur Gafke's book *Pray the Seasons: Pastoral Prayers for Seasons of the Year and of Life*, offers refreshing prayers related to both the Christian Year and the secular calendar. Look through this or another resource that gives you some words for everyday communication with your Creator.

FOUR

Coming To Us

<o>

Advent—The four weeks before December 25

PETER REFLECTS ON THE STORM:

I NEVER LIKED HAVING to fess up to my blunders and failings—and those have been plenty, given how often I jump in without knowing what I'm getting into! So it was a huge relief when I found out from the Teacher that God is willing to forgive us and give us a new start—every day, if need be.

Our times have plenty of things that aren't right; I wonder if it will always be like that. I've found out the hard way that it's better if we just admit our missteps and ask the One who can forgive us to help us put them right. But I'm often reluctant to do that. So here's the amazing thing: Jesus says God doesn't wait for us to get our lives all in order! Our Redeemer comes to rescue us, to help us turn around, and to love us in the process, wherever we are.

<o>

WHILE MANY OF US approach each secular Christmas season with joy, we are also looking for something more. We hope to refresh spiritually. We want to know God in Christ more fully. But this

29

takes place at the very time of the year when our "To Do" lists are longest and our time commitments are stretched to the limit.

Or at least that *was* the case, before a virus enforced isolation and then uncertain social interactions upon us. Gone was the frantic holiday obligation of rushing from one place to another following a too-full social calendar—or else of hiding out in regret, sequestered with our memories of past holidays. A large percentage of people around the globe are no longer in mandatory isolation because of health dangers these days. However, our memories of those past days urges us to reprioritize the whirlwind holiday rush. We may make half-hearted commitments to social engagements that may have merely cluttered our time before the pandemic.

None of us can hope to perpetuate our pre-pandemic routines and conditions. The sea has shifted from gentle swells to a raging tsunami, with surprising lulls and sudden surges. Whatever our outward appearance, we are all "at sea."

This new situation gives us the chance to view the use of our time from a different perspective. What is worth our investment of time, day after day, in the light of our precious, limited life on Earth? Now could be a truly new beginning by rearranging our priorities.

Advent is the first worship season of the "different calendar" called the Christian Year. Formally instituted at the end of the fifth century, it's a time to personally prepare to honor the birth of Jesus Christ, who is both fully divine but also fully human. The word *Advent* means "coming." It refers to the coming of God as Jesus, a flesh and blood person who lived among us and continues to be with us as the Risen Christ.

Granted, most people in Europe and the Americas experience time from past to present to future. But the season of Advent brings God's intended future, God's vision, into our present experience. It often comes to us from unexpected people and places in our lives. Advent calls us to pay attention to a fuller life shown through Jesus' priorities and living presence: a new, faith-filled way of living now.

During Advent, we hear God's message of hope, even as we admit the ways we have failed to be caring, compassionate, or just. At the same time, Advent reminds us of Christ's final coming at the end of history, to transform all that we know into "a new heaven and a new earth."

Advent begins four Sundays before Christmas day. In the fourth century CE, Christians declared it as a time to prepare for Christmas, just as Lent does for Easter. It's a time of expecting Jesus' birth, preparing for Christ's return, and anticipating God's final redemption. In contrast to what likely used to be our pre-Christmas rush of buying and socializing, Advent invites us to slow down and reflect on our lives. Where have we fallen short? How can we live more simply? What would it be like to make more room in our lives for the love of Christ?

THEME 1: Actively Waiting

In the days counting up to Christmas, many people wait with a sense of promise: anticipating our greater welcome to Christ in our lives, our hearts, and our world. In fact, the inspiration for the secular figure of Santa Claus is based on Saint Nicholas, a Christian who honored Jesus Christ above all.

St. Nicholas' love of children and generosity to the poor have given rise to dozens of legends. He was born in the year 270 CE in the coastal town of Patara, in Asia Minor (present day Syria). His parents died in an epidemic when he was a young man, so he began to use his inheritance to help people who were in dire straits. When he heard about a merchant who had lost everything, Nicholas paid the dowries for his three daughters, thereby becoming the patron saint of young women. After a voyage by ship, he aided some sailors and was made their patron saint, as well. Known in Holland as Sinta Klaes (in England and America, Santa Claus), his generosity and his love of children has sparked stories all around the world. He demonstrated Christ's compassion by the way that he lived.

But if Christ is always among us, what are we waiting for in the Advent season? The wait gives us time to reflect on what we need to work on from our side, not what God should be doing for us. We can use the month before Christmas for personal preparation: to take more care in our relationships, to be alert to helping neighbors and strangers, and to thoughtfully shepherd our personal ethics.

This need to ponder and confess our failings also includes admitting the times we were willing to stand mute in the face of a larger system of inequality or injustice. Eli Wiesel, Romanian-born American writer, was an eleven-year-old boy when he entered Auschwitz, where he lost his entire family. "We must always take sides," he said. "Neutrality [always] helps the oppressor, never the victim. Silence encourages the tormentor, never the tormented."

In this current time, many people have experienced a perfect storm of disruption and despair. Even as the first wave of COVID-19 unleashed itself on the world, U.S. citizens' smartphones showed killings of unarmed African Americans by the police throughout the country. Advent calls on us to acknowledge the racism and underlying violence in the fabric of our lives. It challenges our presumed neutrality toward the systems that have kept these iniquities in place.

Theme 2: Living More Simply

How can the Advent season help us live more meaningfully now? It can urge us to radically cast off less meaningful expectations that clutter our lives—as Mary and Joseph must have done with the sudden news of a baby to be born and the revelation that went with it. You can bet how drastically they had to reorder their priorities!

One thing we can do to live more simply is to get rid of all the extra "stuff" that has accumulated in our lives. Many seniors discover they have to "downsize" in order to move into a smaller space. But people of any age can find a freedom in letting go of all sorts of extraneous things they're holding onto. These can be anything from outdated behaviors to Uncle Harvey's old buffalo coat.

The fact is that millions of us have houses full of stuff. We have garages our cars can't fit into because the space is already full. In recent years, an entire industry of self-storage has sprung up, and we actually pay rent to store stuff our houses and garages cannot hold.

A popular trend emerged when Marie Kondo, Japanese professional organizer, popularized her method of decluttering. Hold up the item, she says, and ask yourself, "Is this an absolute necessity? Does this bring me joy?" If not, get rid of it.

If that's true about physical things, what about the non-physical: our attitudes, habits, perspectives and opinions? What "hoarding" of ideas and complacencies have cluttered up our minds, our loyalties, our preoccupations?

THEME 3: Making Room

When a couple finds out they're going to have a baby, suddenly it's important to make room in their house or apartment for the little one to come. It also pushes them to "make room" in their personal and family lives. Suddenly the needs of that tiny baby will have to come first. The same is true of the Advent season—it calls us to make room for Jesus to come first in our actions, habits, and hearts.

In these four weeks before Christmas Day, many of us find our mailboxes stuffed with manger-scene Christmas cards depicting Mary, Joseph, and baby Jesus. I'm wary of the sentimentalized image of a sweet babe surrounded by cooing doves and little lambs. That focus on Jesus in the nativity can keep us from appreciating the reality of what God promised—and delivered—a real human being who grew up to become a strong, passionate, vulnerable human being. Jesus reveals the personhood of God living right in the midst of us, challenging, comforting, and loving us. The traditional church phrase is that he is "God incarnate"—meaning God in human flesh—the One who ultimately fulfills Jewish prophecy and whose life, ministry, death, and Resurrection have reoriented much of human history.

QUESTIONS:

1. What are the pre-Christmas habits and rituals I have developed over the years? Do they include worship services, shopping, parties, caroling, cards, gifts? What are the benefits of each of these activities? Are there ways I could change any of them to fit my new social reality, health standards, and financial concerns? What new habits might be more appropriate in their place?
2. Considering the Advent themes, what changes can I make in my attitudes and actions? What can I let go of to get rid of the clutter of conflicting loyalties I've been carrying? Where can I make a difference to one person in the complex social system in which I live?
3. The Advent perspective challenges many aspects of "me-in-the-center" daily living. How might I gain a different viewpoint on some of the things I do? If Christ is to come into my life in a more meaningful way, how can I shift my priorities to let him in?

THINGS TO DO:

1. Light the candle on your dinner table and say:Candlelighter: "Prepare the way of the Lord."All at the table: "Make room in your heart for the Healer of the nations."
2. Special days in the Advent season provide many opportunities for individual celebrations, beginning with the four Sundays in Advent. Lighting a single candle in a window or on a table the first Sunday, two the second Sunday, and so forth can remind us of Christ, the Light of the world. If a child lives in your home, you can read texts such as John 1: 1–5 or John 8:12. Talk about the

difference Jesus has made in so many lives across time and around the world. Discuss the "light" his followers can bring to the world by showing caring for people, especially those who are often forgotten.

3. "Hanging of the Greens" is a centuries-old tradition that appears in many cultures. It's done at the beginning of Advent to prepare the worship space—in this case your home—for the meanings of the season. Some evergreen branches remind Christians of Christ's promise of life and growth. While mistletoe today is associated with romance, in ancient times it was a symbol of peace. When enemies met under it, they declared a truce. So it reminds Christians today of the peace of God and Christ's power of healing. Some of the first European colonists in America brought the tradition of a Christmas tree with them. A creche, or nativity scene, visually tells the story of Jesus' birth in a stable.

4. An Advent calendar can help you count down the twenty-four days before Christmas Day. The double-layered paper shows a Christmas scene and has numbered windows cut in it. Use or make an Advent Calendar so you and any other members of your household can open a window each day, to see an image related to Christmas or read the next part of the story of Jesus' birth.

5. Or share a section of that original Christmas story once a week and draw a scene or write a poem about the events. Weekly readings could be:
   - The angel's announcement to Mary that she will be with child (Luke 1:26–38),
   - Mary's response of joy and the promise of justice fulfilled (Luke 1:46–55),
   - The birth of Jesus (Luke 2:1–7), and

- The angels' songs of praise and the shepherds' joy (Luke 2:8–20).
- Then on Christmas Eve read about Jesus Christ as God's Word and the Light of the world (John 1:1–14).

6. Research and make Christmas gifts that emphasize time and relationships. Examples could be handmade cards or toys, certificates to redeem for special places to explore together, or a proposed creative project to do together in the year ahead.

7. Learn more about St. Nicholas and related Santa traditions in various world cultures. If you have children at home, talk with them about what St. Nicholas did for others. Choose a local project where you can help people, showing his same spirit in the Advent season.

8. You may plan to have a Christmas tree or a branch to hang ornaments in your home for the Christmas season. "Chrismons" are ornaments in the shape of Christian symbols, to remind you of the meanings of the Christmas season. Here is a recipe to make Chrismons that can last for several years:

For 30 ornaments—10 minutes prep time—1 hour to cook

If you're looking for some new symbols, you can type in "Christian symbols for Christmas," or get a book of Christian symbols from your church or public library.

When you're ready to bake, preheat the oven to 300 degrees F. Mix together 4 c. flour and 1 c. salt. Slowly pour in 1½ c. of water, then mix it with your hands. Knead it until it is soft, about five minutes. Put the dough between two large pieces of parchment paper and roll it out to about 1/8 inch thickness. Remove the top sheet of parchment.

With the dough still on the parchment, cut your shapes out and peel away the extra dough. Some Chrismons might be in the shape of cookie cutters, such as a star, cross, egg, or wreath. Other symbols include an empty tomb, pomegranate, lily, phoenix, peacock, and butterfly. Draw these or other designs with your knife.

Then use a straw to poke a hole in each ornament for hanging. Put the Chrismons on parchment in a baking pan. Bake for 1 hour, or until they are hard.

Once the Chrismons have cooled, you can paint them. To ensure the ornaments last, spray them with a light coat of polyurethane spray (from a hardware or art store). Thread a ribbon through them to be ready to hang on your tree.

FIVE

A Shocking Presence

————◀◦▶————

Christmas

CHRISTMAS—CHRISTMAS DAY THROUGH JANUARY 5

PETER REFLECTS ON THE STORM:

SO THERE WE WERE in that boat altogether, while the four of us fishermen tried to keep the craft upright in that raging sea. Then suddenly someone cried out, "It's a ghost!" Sure enough, to our amazement, someone was walking on the surface of the water!

But then the apparition said, "Take heart, it is I—I Am! Do not fear." I recognized his voice, and his telling us not to be afraid. And finally his unique use of the Sovereign's Sacred Name, given to our great ancestor, Moses.

It was Jesus, all right! I didn't need to check with anyone else in the boat; I knew he was real and coming toward us. I just knew his presence would make all the difference in the world.

————◀◦▶————

D O ANY OF THE FOLLOWING snapshots of Christmas sound familiar? Getting up before dawn to finish that "easy to assemble" present for the kids; bustling in the kitchen with a crowd of friends or family;

tearing open all the packages; devouring the meal; talking a mile a minute to catch up with everyone; then finally collapsing on the couch happy but exhausted, grateful that they're all going home? For many families, that was the "before" picture. Our current picture is apt to look very different. We have lost people during the pandemic: coworkers, friends, family. No one is untouched.

But even before the pandemic, for many of us such a happy "before" picture was more imagined ideal than reality. Some had far fewer family members or friends, far less food to share, far fewer presents to give. Some people hid out, dealing with painful memories or lack of personal connection, perhaps imagining that everyone else "had it all."

But whatever Christmas Day was, it isn't that now. Even if we can gather with others, in most places we are actively aware of sickness and vulnerability. Of those who have survived, fewer people sit at our tables than before the pandemic. Some loved ones have died because of the plague. Some people are still afraid to travel, or simply got out of the habit of leaving their homes. Some family members are fearful of being out among people for very long or without their masks. Others are offended because those once close to them insist on wearing masks or on keeping their distance. Still others feel alienated because of political arguments about how the pandemic happened in the first place or who, if anyone, is to blame.

One thing remains the same, though. For people in a more secular setting, Christmas has been viewed as just one day, perhaps preceded with considerable preparation and anticipation, but one blow-out day, nonetheless. Then all the ornaments got boxed up and put away. Even if a few folks kept the lights up until New Year's Day, basically Christmas was over by December 26. It was time to return to usual routines.

But here is a different reality. In Christian history and current worship, Christmas is an entire season. Christmas Day is just the *beginning* of it, not the culmination. Remember the song, "The Twelve Days of Christmas?" Instead of its being about twelve days (of shopping) *before* Christmas Day, it describes Christmas Day and the eleven days *after*, when we celebrate the fullness of the Good News. We'll explore more about that song later, but the point is that we have more than one day to celebrate God-With-Us. We have an entire, significant season!

The date of December 25 was when non-Christians in Rome held their winter festival to worship the sun. Since Christians refused to worship Caesar or the sun, their special days could have made them stand out as traitors to Rome. So that made December 25 an excellent time for Christians to celebrate Jesus' birth, hidden in the midst of the pagan activities. That date for Jesus' birth was first mentioned about 354 CE. But whatever date they could have chosen, its focus has remained true: that Jesus is God's Word in human form, the Light of the world, who conquers all darkness.

THEME 1: Good News?

It's a good thing Christmas is more than hearing decked-out cherubic choirs, since group singing became known as a dangerous sport. In fact, all coming together for congregational religious events may not be taken for granted any given year, since variants may keep popping up like the flu.

Depending on where we live, we may see Santa look-alikes at stores, and windows glowing brightly with colorful displays. But true Christmas has always been the heart of the matter: what happens inside a person in their relationship with God through Christ, and how they choose to live as a result.

Despite the outer holiday fanfare, Christmas is meant to be the season when we pause to renew our spirits and embrace God's love. It's a time to remember that God has not forgotten this world, that we are not alone, and that God is with us no matter what challenges lie ahead. We can face a new week, month, or year confident that the Healer of the nations has plans of peace for us all.

How do we know this? Even Jesus' name means "God saves." The verb "to save" can mean several actions: to rescue and bring to safety, to keep from becoming spent or lost, to deliver or free, to protect or to preserve. So in Jesus, the Eternal One:

- **Rescues us**—Lifting us out of a sense of meaninglessness or mere survival
- **Finds us**—Reaching out to us through people, events, the Scriptures by enveloping us in love
- **Frees us**—Unlocking us from the chains of isolation and/or animosity we have wrapped around ourselves or others
- **Protects us**—Giving us faith (which means "trust") to praise God, whatever the situation

- **Preserves us**—Offering us joy in compassion, the mutuality of giving and receiving, and strength to strive for justice and service

Life can be tough, even in usual times. Jesus' life and presence show us a way of living that "saves" us in all of these ways.

THEME 2: God With Us

"O come, O come, Emmanuel," begins one popular Christmas carol. *Emmanuel* is Hebrew for "God with us." It's the name Matthew's Gospel gave for Jesus when the angel told Joseph to wed Mary despite her pregnancy. Long ago, when the people of Judah (Israel's southern kingdom) were threatened, they encountered their Redeemer's saving presence through the birth of a child. (See Isaiah 7:14) Now, in Jesus, the Author of Love became fully present to save people threatened by their own sins.

There is overwhelming awe and joy in both the Why and the How of Christmas. The Why is God's love for us, and the How is through Jesus.

One word Christians have long used for this mystery is describing Jesus as "God Incarnate." *Incarnate* means "in the flesh." It refers to some soaring phrases in the Gospel of John: "And the Word became flesh and lived among us, and we have seen his glory, the glory as of a father's only son, full of grace and truth." (John 1:14)

Six centuries ago, the Protestant reformer Martin Luther described the incarnation of the Almighty in Jesus as "God made small." By this he meant our Divine Advocate coming to us in a way we human beings could comprehend, inviting us to receive God's love.

Here are the highlights of a long-ago Christmas story, a modern parable of unknown origin. It's called "The Man and the Birds," told by Paul Harvey on the radio since the 1950s:[1]

Once there was a man who thought Christmas was a lot of humbug. He wasn't a bad person; he was kind and decent toward people. But he didn't believe all that stuff about the Incarnation that churches proclaim at Christmas.

"I'm sorry to distress you," he told his wife, "but I simply cannot understand that claim that God became human. It doesn't make any sense to me."

So on Christmas Eve, his wife and children went off to church without him. "I'll stay at home," he said, "but I'll wait up for you."

Soon after his family left, snow began to fall. And the snow kept falling, getting thicker and heavier. After a while he left his vigil at the window and went back to reading his paper in his chair by the fire.

A few moments later, he heard a thudding sound at the front door. And then another, and another. When he went to the front door to investigate, he found a flock of birds huddled miserably in the snow at his doorstep. "I can't let these poor creatures lie here and freeze," he said to himself. So he put on his coat and boots and tramped out through the snow to the barn. He opened the door wide and turned on the light.

But the birds stayed where they were.

I bet they'll follow food," he thought, so he trudged back to the house to get a bunch of bread crumbs, which he sprinkled on the snow to make a trail to the barn. But the birds ignored the bread and continued to shiver helplessly in the cold.

So the man tried to shoo the birds into the barn by walking around them and waving his arms. But they just scattered in all directions.

"They find me a strange and terrifying creature," he said to himself. "If I could just be a bird myself, maybe I could show them the way to safety."

At that moment the church bells rang.

He sank to his knees in the snow. "Now I understand," he whispered. "Now I see why You had to do it."

THEME 3: The Twelve Days of Christmas

The Christmas season is more than a time to explore why God came into human form to lead us. It's also a time to recall how a Christian can decide to live, assured that we can draw on our Sustainer and Redeemer for strength and purpose.

For example, in that ancient song about the twelve days of Christmas, each element can have a second, deeper meaning:

The partridge in a pear tree is Jesus Christ.
Two turtle doves are the Old and New Testaments.
Three French hens stand for faith, hope, and love.
The four calling birds are the four Gospels: Matthew, Mark, Luke, and John.
Five golden rings recall the Torah, Law or "Teaching," the first five books of the Old Testament.

The six geese a-laying stand for the six days of creation.
Seven swans a-swimming are the seven gifts of the Holy Spirit:
prophesy, serving, teaching, exhortation,
giving, leadership, and mercy.
The eight maids a-milking are the eight beatitudes, "Blessed are"
statements. (Matthew 5:3–12)
Nine ladies dancing are the nine fruits of the Holy Spirit:
love, joy, peace, patience, kindness, goodness, faithfulness, gentle-
ness, and self-control.
The ten lords a-leaping are the Ten Commandments.
Eleven pipers piping stand for the eleven faithful disciples.
The twelve drummers drumming symbolize the twelve
points of belief in the Apostles' Creed.

With this song, people don't have to be able to read or have
books beyond the Bible to get all the hallmarks of a moral
life. We can sing the song and know important guidelines for
Christian living.

QUESTIONS:

1. What aspect of Jesus' name would I like to explore, to
   experience more joy? How would I like to go beyond a
   sense of mere survival?
2. How can "God with us" or the story of the birds in the
   snow help us understand Jesus Christ?
3. How could knowing about the twelve days of Christmas
   after Christmas Day influence my perspective? Which
   day's meaning would I like to explore further? Faith,
   hope, or love; one of the Gospels, perhaps; or a specific
   gift of the Holy Spirit?

Things To Do:

1. Light the candle on your dinner table and say:Candle-lighter: "God is with us, Emmanuel."All at the table: "Even in the worst of times, the Giver of Life surrounds and upholds us."

2. If you send out Christmas cards to people, think about how Christ is the heart of Christmas. In your message, see how you can express more than just what happened to your family this past year. Pray for the people who will receive the card, and then add a note that gives them truly good news.

3. When you hear Christmas music, listen for the real Christmas story within it, such as in Handel's *Messiah* or in many Christmas carols.

4. Remember Christmas is Jesus' birthday! Bake a cake and sing "Happy Birthday." Give a gift to others by offering your time, abilities, or money to an organization that cares for the earth, saves animals, or meets an important human need.

5. Draw or cut out pictures of one or more symbols of the season. Write a short story or poem that uses it in your writing.

6. Set aside a day for reflection sometime during the Christmas season. This can be done on any day. You can invite family members, friends, or neighbors to do this at the same time in their own homes. The purpose of the day is to "be still and know that I am God." (Psalm 46:10) At the beginning you might read John 1:1–4 or a version of the Christmas story. Rest in awareness of your Loving Parent. Think about how you have served Christ over this past year. Ask forgiveness for your shortcomings. You may choose to end the day by singing familiar lines from your favorite Christmas carols.

SIX

Looking Forward

————◄o►————

Epiphany

EPIPHANY—JANUARY 6 UNTIL ASH WEDNESDAY

PETER REFLECTS ON THE STORM:

WHEN YOU'RE IN A STORM it's important to keep an eye on the details, in case something minor turns lethal. But that's a defensive posture. Once I'd figured out that it really *was* Jesus walking on the water, I quit worrying about survival. Instead, I focused my eyes on Jesus. What was he doing out there? If he could do that, maybe I could, too.

Some people keep their faith really private, either to protect themselves or because they think faith has nothing to do with the world. But one thing we had learned about the Teacher: he *loves* the world! Almost every day he's up before dawn, ready to heal and spread the Word to strangers, to learn from them and to bring God's light more brightly into their lives. His presence shines a light not only on who he is, but also on who we are and can be.

Especially in the wildest, scariest times, that's the kind of person I want to be with! He really is the Light of the world.

————◄o►————

JANUARY AND FEBRUARY can be a quiet time of the year for many people. It also can have a morning-after feeling from overdoing Christmas and New Year's celebrations. Those initial months can be a time of regret. "Did I spend too much on gifts this year? Did I go to one too many parties?" Those days can feel like a long, dreary stretch between the cold of midwinter and the warmth of spring.

The season of Epiphany, however, holds plenty to explore and to learn. Beginning on January 6, it can last from four to nine weeks until Ash Wednesday, the first day of Lent. During this time, people in the Eastern Church (Coptic Christians in Africa, and all the Orthodox denominations) focus on Jesus' birth and baptism. Meantime, we in the "Western Church" (Christians in Europe, North and South America, and most countries west of Russia) associate Epiphany primarily with the story of the Magi, or wise ones, who came from the East to honor the baby Jesus.

The arrival of the Magi is known as the first time non-Jewish people, Gentiles, had a chance to hear the Good News about God's presence and purpose in Jesus. So for all Christians around the globe, the Epiphany season shows us who He is and the difference He can make in our lives.

The word *epiphany* means a "manifestation," "revelation," or "appearance," particularly of something divine. In the Christmas season we recognize Jesus himself as God's epiphany, the Incarnate One. Now this season of Epiphany takes the concept further. It points out different ways Jesus shows us the mystery of divine love, and how we can show such care in return, particularly through missions around the globe.

The day of Epiphany is also called "Three Kings Day" in many Latin American countries, including Mexico, Spain, the Dominican Republic, and Hispanic communities in the United States, as well as in Germany and France. The night before Three Kings Day, many children leave out their empty shoes or stuff hay in boxes under their beds to attract the wise ones' camels. When they wake up the next morning they find presents. Families also celebrate with a Kings Cake that contains a hidden nut, coin, or little toy inside it. (See "Things to Do" at the end of this chapter for a simple recipe.) The day can include nativity scenes, holiday songs, and festive lights in the streets, along with a joyful parade of the kings, who arrive on horseback or on elaborate floats.

The major image for the Epiphany season is that of light. "Arise, shine, for your light has come," God says, inviting all people scattered around the world to come home. (Isaiah 60:1–3) We can reflect the light of our Maker and also draw strength from it. As John 1:3–5 states, "The light shines in the darkness, and the darkness did not / cannot overcome it!" The Greek verb is ongoing, showing that the light will always overcome the power of darkness.

Another frequent emphasis during Epiphany is the worldwide community of faith and Christian mission around the globe. We are "all in the same boat" as human beings, utterly dependent on God's grace and forgiveness. When Jesus told us to help people who are marginalized and are treated as "the least" around us, he did not say to stop at government borders. Time and again, his earthly life and ministry demonstrated global care. We are to "let our light shine" like a lamp in the house, like a city on a hill. (Matthew 5:14–16)

The image of light used throughout Epiphany builds on the foundation that Jesus is the Word made flesh (John 1:14) and the "Light of the world" (John 8:12). That is the core message of the Christmas season. The Bible passages read each year during Epiphany show people reflecting Christ's light to others. Epiphany becomes an invitation to move from fear to hope, trusting in the reality of the One who made all that lives.

Three epiphanies, or manifestations, of Christ are described during this season. The first is the coming of the Magi, the wise ones from the East. Second is Jesus' own baptism. And third is Jesus' first miracle: turning water into wine at Cana of Galilee.

THEME 1: Follow the Star

The first "epiphany," or appearance, of Christ in the world is at his birth in Bethlehem. It's the story of the *Magi*, those wise ones who journeyed from the East to bring gifts to the baby Jesus. Historically they were probably priests in Zoroastrianism and the earlier religions of western Iran. If so, they practiced astrology, astronomy, alchemy, and other forms of esoteric knowledge. At that time astrologers were highly respected among the Greeks, whose culture was then considered the apex of civilization. But such "seers" were definitely *not* valued in either Testament of the Bible. So whoever they were, the wise ones were seen as outside the realm of respectable Jewish society. This fact foreshadows Jesus' life-long emphasis on associating with and caring for people left out by those who are the "high and mighty."

LOOKING FORWARD • 53

It is not remarkable that these wise ones were watching the sky, but it was amazing that they saw a *moving* star and followed it into regions of the world unknown to them to search out its meaning. So what about that actual star? Modern astronomers speculate that the phenomenon might have been a lunar eclipse that took place on the planet Jupiter on April 17 in the year 6 BCE. So the Star of Bethlehem could have been a traceable celestial phenomenon.

For a minute, picture the journey those Magi would have undertaken: the perilous, long trek at the coldest time of year, their camels sore-footed, and the camel drivers grumbling and periodically running away. Their night fires must have sputtered against the dark, their only shelter a blanket. Then imagine the hostility of the townsfolk once these looked-down-upon foreigners got into Jewish territory. In the end, no doubt they preferred traveling at night, sleeping in snatches, trying to ignore any daytime onlookers who sneered at their folly.

What God had given to the Magi was the star itself, the beacon of their curiosity and persistence. But Divine Wisdom also gave them an openness to learning more about the world, and a willingness to risk everything for the sake of their vision.

At first, what they received from other people was derision and danger. Expecting to herald the birth of a new king, they naturally sought out the royal palace. There, they asked a powerful question—but it was the wrong place to get a truthful answer. Yes, Herod was a Jew by birth, but he worshiped multiple deities and would hardly have welcomed a rival king.

Inquiring of the man officially named by Rome as the King of the Jews, the Magi asked where the newborn King of the Jews could be found. Herod consulted his own seers (in themselves a sign of his belief in other gods). They pointed the travelers in the general direction of Bethlehem. Herod told the travelers to return to the palace to inform him exactly where the royal child was. His purpose, of course, was to execute this unexpected rival, not to honor him.

The story in Matthew 2 tells us that the wise ones gave the child three unusual gifts. Looking back, people of faith say those odd gifts made sense:

- Gold, the symbol of royalty and sign of wealth
- Frankincense, a fragrant incense, long used as a symbol for prayer to the Eternal One
- Myrrh, the substance used to embalm bodies at death, anticipating Jesus' willing gift of his own life on the cross

The fact that the Magi were Gentiles signaled from the beginning that Jesus had come into the world for everyone. Later generations like ours know his presence was meant to give new life to the Jews, and also to people from every nation around the globe.

Thankfully, God had warned the Magi in a dream that they needed to get home by an alternate route. By acting on that dream, they gave the baby Jesus one more gift: his life. Their refusal to return to Herod allowed Joseph enough time to take Mary and the baby down to Egypt, thereby saving the One who would ultimately save us all.

THEME 2: Jesus' Baptism

The second event that reveals who Jesus is came when his cousin John baptized him. (Matthew 3:13–17; Mark 1:9–11) Matthew's story says John recognized Jesus' greater authority. John asked why Jesus came to him to be baptized, and not the other way around. Jesus' response was that it needed to be that way "for now," to "fulfill all righteousness." In that event, Jesus saw the Holy Spirit descending upon him. Then he heard the Divine Voice call him a beloved Son.

Today, people may be baptized as children or as adults, according to different church traditions. They may do it by sprinkling water, pouring water over the head, or fully immersing the person. However people are baptized, they join the universal Body of Christ, no matter what denomination or group performs the rite.

In worship today, most churches baptize primarily babies and children. Those congregations emphasize the importance of bringing them up in the Christian faith, encouraging the parents to raise their young ones by their words and by example. Many parents also choose an exemplary person or couple to be "godparents" to the child as s/he grows up. The congregation also plays an important part, promising to help guide the child in Christlike living. The full fruit of baptism is both a personal trust in God and faithful participation in the life of a faith community.

In some churches only adults are baptized. This is the pattern in the New Testament: baptism only after the person has proclaimed his or her personal faith. In biblical times and the early centuries thereafter—and in some places in the world today—becoming a Christian meant potentially being persecuted, arrested, or killed by the government or other religious authorities. So it was essential for those being baptized to understand what they were promising. They made an explicit confession of faith, aware of the risk they were taking. In these adult-confession churches, children are "dedicated" or "blessed" instead. The ritual is an act of commitment by the parents to raise the child in a way that follows Jesus.

Whether the one baptized is a child or an adult, baptism can mean several things. First, it is a sacrament—"an outward and visible sign of an inward and spiritual grace." It means the outward gesture does not have meaning in itself. It symbolizes the real thing: that God is at work inside the one being baptized. God's grace initiates an intimate, personal connection and commitment..

Baptism is also a covenant: a relationship and personal promise that our God makes to the person receiving baptism. It names the unique individual as entering into the embrace of the One who offers forgiveness to us all.

At the same time, baptism is a channel for the Holy Spirit to create a faith community, generation after generation. It reminds us of the God's presence, including in times of vulnerability. No matter how lonely or isolated we may feel, we are never alone.

Finally, baptism points to both the future and the "now," reminding us to keep growing in grace, as we learn to live in a more Christ-like way. It assures us that in every present moment the Giver of new life can give us a fresh start, as if we were born anew.

THEME 3: Wine for the Wedding

The third epiphany, or revelation, of Jesus in this worship season took place in the Galilean town of Cana. (John 2:1–11) It happened at a wedding, when Jesus turned water for foot washing into the finest wine.

Back then, wedding celebrations lasted for an extended time, which meant hosting guests over a number of days. Jesus and his disciples had been invited, as well as his mother. Not surprisingly, the wine ran out. Mary spoke to Jesus about it. Maybe that was because all those disciples had imbibed a great deal of it, or because she knew from the angel that her son was able to do unusual things. In any case, when the last drop was drained, she approached Jesus.

"Woman," Jesus said (a term of formal respect), "what concern is that to you and to me? My hour has not yet come." Here Jesus was referring to the "hour" when the religious leaders would see him for who he was and would decide to eliminate him as a threat. Clearly this comment reveals the human side of Jesus, not wanting to be exposed before the intended time.

But Mary knew her son well and was confident he would do something to fix the situation. She also must have held some stature in that home or in the community, because she went to the household servants and said, "Do whatever he tells you."

In those days, everyone except the rich traveled by foot. No matter who you were in that arid land, travel was a long, dusty affair. So families kept large containers of water standing just inside the front door to wash the feet of weary guests. Among the people of Israel, foot washing was not just a matter of hospitality; it was also an act of purification in their religion.

After being confronted about the wine, Jesus changed his mind. Six large, stone jars were standing in that house for the Jewish rite of foot washing. Each jar could hold twenty or thirty gallons: a great abundance, indeed.

"Fill the jars with water," Jesus said. The servants poured

water up to the brim. Then he said, "Now draw some out, and take it to the chief steward." So they did.

The chief steward was the person in charge of everything going on in the household, managing events on behalf of the homeowner. That included anything that might go wrong hosting the community during this celebration. It meant the wine problem was his problem.

When the chief steward tasted the water, it had become wine! John reminds us that he didn't know where the wine had come from, although the servants knew. The chief steward took a glass of the new wine to the bridegroom and said, "Everyone serves the good wine first, and then the inferior wine after the guests have become drunk. But you have kept the good wine until now!"

So how does this event show us something deep and true about Jesus? Jesus himself is the best wine of all! His supreme value is not only in what he does for all people, but in who he is: the fullness of our sovereign, loving God, translated into a fully human person. As Psalm 34 declares, "Taste and see that the Lord is good!"

The fact that this superior wine was given at a wedding feast is significant for people familiar with the Bible. Passages in Matthew 22 and 25 describe joy at the end of time. It is like a wedding feast when Christ will marry God's creation. Everyone will share in the rich banquet of God's love. The wedding-feast setting of the story is a potent reminder of eternal life awaiting us at the fulfillment of human history.

Questions:

1. Are there places in my life where I have seen an expression of God's love, shown through Christ or through another person? What have been the signs of God's "Light" shining through even my darkest days? Here's

a space to write down some key times when I felt the God around me:

_____

_____

_____

2. If I think of myself as on a journey, what can I learn from those Magi? What gifts has God given to me? What trappings might I need to discard for the journey? What is the distinct "star" that is trying to catch my attention to lead me forward? What might be the different road by which I am meant to return home?
3. Have I ever experienced "an inward and spiritual grace?" If so, what form has it taken: making a covenant or vow, receiving or giving forgiveness, becoming part of a spiritual community, looking forward to an eternal future?
4. If Jesus is metaphorically "the best wine of all," are there other substitutes that I have tried? How do the alternatives compare? What values affect my judgment?

THINGS TO DO:

1. Light the candle on your dinner table and say:

    CANDLELIGHTER: "Jesus Christ is the Light of the world."
    ALL AT THE TABLE: "The Light shines in the darkness and nothing can overcome it".

2. On the day of Epiphany, people in many Latin American countries celebrate *Dia de Los Reyes,* or "Three Kings Day." In honor of that day, you may want

to make a King Cake. If you're an expert baker you can do the long, three- or four-hour version. But if you'd like a quick, easy recipe to do with your little ones, you can make a Kings Cake this way:

Ingredients:

2 cans of refrigerated Cinnamon Rolls with Butter Cream (for a cinnamon sugar flavor) or Grands plus frosting from the store. This usually makes sixteen rolls.

Colored sugar –Green is best because it's the color of the season. But if you can't find that color, use any multi-colored cake sprinkles.

One almond or pecan, tiny crown, or plastic toy baby (to look like the baby Jesus hiding from Governor Herod).

Instructions:

a) Preheat the oven to 375 degrees F. Grease or line a cookie sheet, then arrange the rolls sideways so they form a circle.

b) Bake according to the instructions on the package, then let them cool.

c) Use buttercream to frost the entire top of the cinnamon rolls. Then sprinkle each half of the cake top with the green sprinkles OR by alternating purple sugar, no sugar (leaves a band of white frosting), and green sugar. This pattern matches the worship seasons in each cycle of the Christian year. OR with the multicolored cake sprinkles. Talk about how (like the purple, white and green for the worship seasons) we are always preparing, celebrating, and growing in God's love.

d) Serve the King Cake immediately and tell your family or guests that something is hidden inside. Whoever gets the hidden treasure is honored king or queen for the day and gets to wear a paper crown at dinner. OR s/he gets to make the next major meal for everyone (often tamales). OR s/he can bring the next King Cake in another twelve days to keep the twelve-day tradition going.

3. Have you ever been baptized? If not, is there any reason you would want to do that? If some event has changed you or you have a new understanding of its meaning, you can be baptized or renew your baptism at this time.

4. You don't have to talk about Jesus to share the love of Christ. This Epiphany season, you could volunteer in the Big Brothers Big Sisters organization, in Scouting, or in another youth organization. What would help young people most in your area, that fits with your "mission" right around you?

5. Epiphany day is a perfect time to start planning a play based on the adventures of the Magi. If you have nearby children, this is especially fun to put on for your neighbors. Get four refrigerator boxes from a nearby appliance store, to paint as back-drop scenery. By revolving the cartons simultaneously, you can create four different scenes to use in turn. "Stage hands" behind the boxes can change the scenery in plain view of the audience. The audience often is so delighted when the scenes change that they applaud the scenery! You can add crowning a "king" and "queen" of the event, and anything else you would like to make the day delightful.

6. Some churches use Epiphany to hold mission studies for different age levels, to learn more about Jesus' ongoing work through the Church around the globe. You can do this within your family, as well. Once a

week, point out a country on an Internet map. Next, search for "ministry in [name of country]." Then give thanks for the good things going on there.

7. One special way to celebrate Epiphany is to gather "white gifts:" practical presents wrapped in plain, white paper, so no one knows which are more or less expensive. They can be given to local people who are homeless or in other situations of need. Begun in 1904 in Painesville, Ohio, White Sunday has become popular in Canada and the U.S. It can be any day of the week and is a fun way to involve your neighborhood or wider community.

SEVEN

Taking Stock

◄○►

Lent

LENT—FROM ASH WEDNESDAY UNTIL THE DAY BEFORE EASTER

PETER REFLECTS ON THE STORM:

OKAY, SO IT WAS PROBABLY a stupid thing to do, asking if I could walk with him in that storm. But Jesus was already out there doing it! How amazing was that? Clearly he could command the elements if he was walking on the water. Asking was a risk, but Jesus is all about risk—at least when it comes to showing God's crazy care for us all. He risks his safety in order to reach out to others, to bring about justice, to show personal compassion. So maybe he wanted to see how much we trusted him? He said, "Come." I took him up on his offer.

Sometimes it takes the greatest courage for us to look inside ourselves and admit how far we are from where we were meant to be. Yeah, I sank really fast, but I know God loves us regardless, and the Teacher was there to rescue me.

◄○►

I F EPIPHANY IS THE SEASON of vision, Lent is a time of reflection. It's a period of embedding God's vision for us in our everyday living. Lent is not a jolly, fun season. It's

63

a pause for thoughtful review, seeing through our illusions, and being honest with God about who we really are. But it is not a time to fill ourselves with neurotic guilt, nor to see how miserable we can make ourselves. The Compassionate One does not want us to wallow in shame. God loves us, and frees us from self-condemnation, when we permit it. Our personal relationship with our Redeemer gives us the courage to look at the less-than-best sides of ourselves and be open to transformation.

Likewise, the purpose of Lent is not to "make amends" (as if we could ever earn our way to heaven). It is to gain more appreciation for what our Redeemer has done for us through Jesus. It can be a time of assessing our goals and lifestyle, wrestling with whatever weighs us down and keeps us from living a vibrant, joyous life. The point is not to "give up" some habit we dearly love, but to give ourselves more fully to God. The Lenten season is an opportunity to turn our lives around, facing our own ambiguities in the light of Truth.

Originally, Lent was a period of fasting and penance for new Christian converts to prepare for baptism on the evening before Easter. It became a time of recommitting loyalty to the one true God over any other authority. That meant dealing with temptation, sin, suffering, and sorrow. By the fifth century, all Christians used the season to prepare for Easter renewal.

Theme 1: Getting Back on Track

Paul Tournier, eminent pastoral counselor and physician, says we are like a boy who receives a beautiful, mechanical toy for Christmas. His father says, "I'll show you how to make it go."

But the boy refuses. "No, I want to do it myself!" He tries to figure it out, but he can't. So he gets angry, takes out his

frustration on the toy, then complains that he can't make it work. He hands it back to his father and says, "You make it work." The father gazes in dismay at the wreckage. By this time the toy is nearly destroyed.

Tournier says the beautiful, very complicated toy is like our life. We insist on trying to make it work on our own, but it keeps going wrong. The more we attempt to force it with our own strength, the more it frustrates us. Finally, in desperation, we may ask our Loving Parent to take over, as we admit defeat.

The problem is we have made the situation worse by trying to fix our lives by ourselves. At that point it has to be repaired before anything can work right. Persistence and petulance on our part will not provide a solution.

What kind of life does God want for us? Micah 6:8 says it's to do justice, love kindness (from the Hebrew literally meaning "steadfast, covenant loyalty"), and to walk humbly with God. But inevitably we wander off track personally and as a people. This is one way of describing "sin:" becoming estranged both vertically and horizontally, and even from our truer selves.

So Lent is a time to admit how we have fallen short and to ask the Healer of our hearts to restore our broken, beautiful lives. "Create in me a clean heart, O God," we say, "and put a new and right spirit within me." (Psalm 51:10) The goal is not to go faster or with more determination, but to "turn around"—the meaning of "repentance" in biblical Hebrew— to live face-to-face once more with the One who gave us birth.

It is never too late for us to enter into a closer relationship with God. Lent reminds us of this. The season helps us set aside a period each year to examine our priorities and admit we want to come home to the One who loves us still. "Yet even now, says the LORD, return to Me with all your heart.... Return to the LORD, your God, for God is gracious and merciful, slow to anger and abounding in steadfast love...." (Joel 2:12–13)

The first day of Lent is called Ash Wednesday. It is a time to reflect on our own mortality and to re-examine ourselves in the light of the horror of the cross and the beauty of the love Jesus showed for us by enduring it. Whatever we choose to do or not do in Lent, it's meant to bring us back to our personal center of gravity in God, and to reaffirm a grateful, humble, and generous heart.

THEME 2: Tending Our Soul

The six weeks of Lent are an excellent time to tend our souls. Your "soul" is your distinctive identity and authentic self, the whole of us that communicates clearly with the Author of our lives. Lent can supply some quiet time in our daily or weekly routines. We can check our inner compass for making the right decisions. We can listen more acutely for the subtle interactions of the Spirit.

Reduced busyness also can help us look into the empty places in our lives, such as our addictions: the privileges, habits, and possessions that we may hang onto so dearly. These can be obvious ones, such as alcohol, smoking, food, or social media addictions. But they can also be subtler drains on our well-being: over-extended family roles, intrusive friendships, power-play patterns with co-workers, clinging to the past, or obsessing about the future. We can get hooked on whatever we use to comfort ourselves or to block out pain and fear. In fact, addictions can be *anything* we try to cram into that hollow place in our lives that only our Creator can fill.

One way to examine our spiritual lives is to use periods of outer silence to ask ourselves questions, such as:

- Why is it hard to love my neighbor? Are there times when I put other people down or try to be superior to them?
- Do I blame my troubles on God? Can I trust that pain and difficulties will never overwhelm the gift of grace?
- What prompts me to try to be Number One? Do I always have to compete with others? Or do I try to be invisible, so I won't get hurt?

We can look from multiple angles at whatever questions emerge. The questions might come from our worship life, from what different Bible texts tell us, or from our experience or relating to others. In the process, we may come to know ourselves a bit better and to be more open to the promptings of the Spirit.

Theme 3: Fasting, Praying, Giving

Fasting, praying, and giving to the poor have been part of Lent from the earliest centuries. As with all spiritual practices, our attitude and intentions—the focus of our heart and mind—are even more important than what we do outwardly.

Fasting

The first of these three Lenten expressions, fasting, at its root, means being "steadfast" or "holding fast." When we hold fast to the Living God in a specific dimension of our lives—whether it's fasting from food or from anything else—we accept how God holds *us* fast. It is a way of trusting the One who refuses to let us go.

Fasting can be a way for the body to quiet down, leaving off all sorts of distractions and surface pleasures. It can be a way of communicating and recognizing our deep dependency not only on God, but also on the creatures around us, with whom we live. But if fasting just prompts me to fixate on a desire for Kentucky Fried Chicken, I've missed the point. I've probably tried to fast without prayer, or attempted to do too much all at once. I need to start with baby steps, increasing the commitment as I progress.

Feeding my face can be as much an emotional issue as a nutritional one, especially when an overabundance of food is available. Eating can be a way of filling the empty places in my life with what I think I can control. So a little self-imposed abstinence can help me notice where I'm getting my day-to-day comfort.

There are no rules for fasting. We might omit one meal, one meal a day, or the meals on one day each week. We may commit to simplifying our eating habits one day a week or for all weekdays. We could give up one big meal a week and donate the money saved to a program that feeds the hungry.

We might quit having between-meal snacks, or something else. The point of giving up is not deprivation; it is to help us remember to *hold fast to* something positive in our lives.

What we fast *from* can be something other than food, as well. I might decide to:

fast *from* bursts of anger in order *to* embrace acts of compassion;

fast *from* bitter thinking *to* a fuller forgiveness;

fast *from* focusing on when I've been wronged *to* celebrate times of joy;

fast *from* discontent *to* hold onto gratitude.

The point is not denial or self-abnegation, but holding onto God's steadfast love for me. I may accept it for only a while, but I know that each small bout of self-discipline can help me develop a longer term habit of grateful being with God.

PRAYING

Fasting naturally links us to prayer—listening for the Holy Spirit, sharing our deepest desires, and paying attention to our attitudes and actions. No matter how we do it, prayer prompts us to rely on our Creator to help us through both external and internal storms.

The way we pray describes our relationship with God. It also offers us the chance to confess we are not the way we want to be with other people. In these moments we can come back to the One who calls us home.

Prayer does not change our natural, first-response reactions to what happens to us. But it helps us recognize those events as times we can experience grace. What matters is not *how* we pray, but that our prayers are alive and sincere.

Our prayer can take many shapes from hour to hour. It may be to wake up to the presence of the Holy Spirit, to open our own hearts and listen for that "still, small voice" within us, to receive divine counsel from a surprising source. It is a way to welcome the Living God into every part of our lives. It is also a way to enter into the heart of the One who loves us all and then pray for others from that perspective of love.

Prayer often clarifies our intentions and hopes, expressing our unvoiced "sighs too deep for words" (Romans 8:26). It can remind us of the pangs we ignore or the longings we deny. It prompts us to think about "whatever is true, whatever is honorable, whatever is just, whatever is pure, whatever is pleasing, whatever is commendable, if there is any excellence and if there is anything worthy of praise." (Philippians 4:8–9)

Above all, for me prayer is messy. It reflects my life in its unfinishedness, with its dark corners and momentary light, and reminds me of God's love through and despite it all.

GIVING

Along with fasting and prayer, Lent also highlights giving time and money that benefits people who are struggling.

Jesus said, "Where your treasure is, there your heart will be also." (Matthew 6:21) That's certainly true! Whenever I make a significant financial gift to a ministry, my "heart" goes right along with it. I feel like an investor in the enterprise. I want to know what happens and how people's lives are being changed. I'm not a million-dollar giver, but whenever the amount is significant for me, it tends to pull my heart in that direction.

This process is what I call the mutuality of giving and receiving. Money is one medium of human relationship, and whenever giving goes on, it can benefit both the giver and the receiver. Lent is an excellent time to find ways to help my nearby neighbors through community programs. It is also a great time to contribute to networks and organizations that alleviate some of the suffering I see in the world.

The old-fashioned word "almsgiving" might bring up terrible images of condescension or extortion. But "alms," from Old English, means "a kind gift for someone in need." Giving and receiving can be done with mutual respect and appreciation. We can give practical help for people in material want, while appreciating the resilience they must have to endure their circumstances.

I experienced this firsthand in a town my ministry took me to live in for one week every month. Instead of leaving the homeless and hungry to fend for themselves on every street corner, a few folks in the community created a network to let those who were homeless choose specific territories where they could sell a weekly newspaper to people who had money to give. The cost of the paper was ten cents or anything more you could donate, and the money would go to the seller of the paper. In return, the newspaper featured stories about the economic dynamics of that town and various factors that affected the homeless. The middle-class readers gained understanding, and the newspaper sellers received money to help make ends meet. The arrangement also encouraged a personal relationship between buyer and seller, since they would see each other regularly at the same location from week to week.

Giving has to do with a lot more than just finances. Giving one's time often can be even more valuable than money for people in economically developed nations. So personal involvement in community service can be a larger commitment. We can help at a food bank or in a cold weather shelter, chaperone children on a field trip, or assist in an after-school program. The possibilities are endless. In many situations we can realize how much we have in common with those who at first seem like the needy ones. We may also glimpse what we can learn from their experience and from their faith.

Fasting, praying, and giving encourage us to live with greater integrity as we try to walk in the way of Jesus.

QUESTIONS:

1. What repetitive patterns do I see in the way I have lived that lead to frustration and broken relationships? What lessons could the Teacher of my soul want me to learn?
2. Where are there empty spaces in my life that I've tried to fill up with something less than the Eternal One? How can I rediscover God's presence in those places?
3. Are there ways in which I could pray, fast, and give that could bring a more balanced or fulfilling relationship with the One who created me?

THINGS TO DO:

1. Light the candle on your dinner table and say:

CANDLELIGHTER: "Create in me a clean heart, O God,"
ALL AT THE TABLE: "and renew a right spirit within me."

2. Look for a Lenten devotional booklet to track your days. For example, Creative Communications for the Parish has produced booklets of daily readings from Henri J.M. Nouwen, C.S. Lewis, and Dietrich

Bonhoeffer. They also have separate booklets of readings for teenagers and for children.

3. Find and use a daily Lenten calendar. Or make a weekly calendar for Lent based on the elements outlined in this chapter. For each of the six weeks of Lent, choose a sentence to ponder, a Bible text, and one of the season's three themes highlighted in this chapter. Keep a journal and spend some time praying about your discoveries.

4. Make pretzels to eat throughout the weeks of Lent. The Christians in Rome used to make them from flour, salt, and water for fasting days. They called them *braceliai*, or "little arms," because the shape looked like arms crossed in prayer. Try this recipe:

3 cups warm milk
1 package dry yeast
1 tsp. salt
1 Tbsp. sugar
¼ cup melted shortening
7 cups flour
1 egg white
Coarse or sea salt

Add yeast to a half cup of the warm milk; stir until dissolved. Add salt, sugar, shortening, flour, and rest of warm milk; mix well. Knead for six to eight minutes until smooth, adding flour if necessary. Place in a bowl, cover, and let it rise for about an hour until doubled. Punch it down and let it rest for 10 minutes.

With floured hands, roll a golf-ball-size piece of dough to a 14- to 16-inch roll. On a cookie sheet, form a pretzel shape, crossing the ends of the roll to look like arms crossed in prayer. Keep pretzels apart. Brush with egg white mixed with a little water. Sprinkle with salt. Let them rise for 30 minutes.

Bake at 400 degrees for 15 minutes. Makes about three dozen pretzels.

5. Chart your own spiritual journey. Turn a sheet of paper crosswise. Halfway down, draw a timeline horizontally across the page, with vertical hash marks reflecting the years or decades of your life. Then plot any major highs and lows above and below the horizontal line and connect them. Devote a regular time to journal or think about what you learned from any of these life experiences. Turn that time into prayer.

EIGHT

A Long Way Down

───◀◉▶───

Holy Week

HOLY WEEK—THE LAST WEEK OF LENT

PETER REFLECTS ON THE STORM:

I COULDN'T BELIEVE IT. Was I really walking on the water? So I looked down just for a second—and caught a glimpse of those wild depths!

At that instant I plunged into the watery chaos. I knew I wouldn't see light or life ever again.

"Lord, save me!" I cried.

Thinking about it now, maybe the crazy thing was not getting out of the boat. It was taking my eyes off Jesus once I was out there.

————◦————

IN THE SECULAR WATERS we swim in, the week before Easter is often filled with positive expectations of the weekend to come. Children and their families anticipate Easter egg hunts, perhaps a new spring outfit, and a big family feast on Easter Sunday. Many look forward to attending a church worship service, as well.

But the week before that first Easter had an entirely different quality for Jesus' disciples. For all of us who came later, the ultimate impact of Easter Sunday is magnified by the roller coaster of highs and lows in Jesus' life that immediately preceded his death.

No one back then could have had any notion Easter was coming, of course. Later generations would form it into a "Holy Week," having witnessed the events that gave it significance. The week began with popular excitement over news of a new king, and ended with a public execution followed by emptiness and grief. But more than suffering and death took place that Holy Week.

The word *holy* in the Old Testament means "set apart," and with good reason. In the midst of human betrayal, the week's events contained successive intimations of God's overwhelming grace. At first, Jesus' triumphal entry revealed him as the Sovereign who serves his people. Then at the Last Supper, the disciples experienced intimacy with our Lord at the table. And finally, on Friday, Jesus embodied divine love that refuses to let us go, even to the point of death.

The events of that singular week seemed anything but holy. In just seven days, Jesus went from being hailed as the king-elect, to being executed as a traitor. There are multiple parallel accounts by Matthew, Mark, and Luke. These are the turning points:

- Sunday: Entering Jerusalem—Jesus comes into the capital city as an alternative event to the governor's arrival—Mark 11:1–10
- Tuesday: Conspiracy against Jesus—The chief priests and elders plan to arrest and kill Jesus—Matthew 26:1–5
- Burial ointments put on Jesus—A woman sneaks into a fancy dinner and pours ointment on his head—Matthew 26:6–13
- Judas plots to betray Jesus—Judas Iscariot offers to give Jesus up to the religious authorities—Matthew 26:17–19
- Wednesday: Preparing for Passover—The disciples secure an "upper room" to celebrate Passover with Jesus—Mark 14:12–16
- Thursday evening: Jesus' last supper—At the *Seder* meal, Jesus reveals that one of the disciples will betray him and the disciples will deny him—Mark 14:17–31
- Thursday night: Agony in Gethsemane—In the garden, Jesus prays, knowing what's coming. The disciples keep falling asleep—Mark 14:36–42
- Thursday night: Jesus is arrested—Judas comes with a crowd to arrest Jesus and identifies him to the authorities with a kiss—Mark 14:43–52
- Thursday night: Peter's denial—Challenged three times, Peter denies he knows Jesus—Luke 22:54–71
- Thursday night: Jesus is brought before the Jewish Council—The religious leaders accuse Jesus of committing blasphemy—Mark 14:53–65

- Friday: Jesus on trial before Pilate—The Council brings Jesus before the Roman governor, demanding the death penalty. The crowd insists Pilate use his pardon to save a violent criminal instead of Jesus—Mark 15:1–15
- Friday: Jesus is crucified and dies on the cross—Pilate sentences Jesus to death by crucifixion: the agonizing death of common criminals. The Roman soldiers mock him, and he is crucified—Mark 15:16–41
- Friday before sundown: Burial of Jesus—Joseph of Arimathea gives his burial cave for Jesus' body. Mary Magdalene and Mary, Jesus' mother, witness where his body is laid to rest —Mark 15:42–47
- On Saturday the disciples all but drown in devastating emptiness saturated with grief.
- But Jesus' *Abba* ("Daddy") wasn't finished yet, and held one more incredible surprise!

Theme 1: Pomp and Circumstance

Rulers in every time and culture have felt the need to impress the people they controlled with both their power and their prestige. Throughout the centuries of the great Roman Empire, political leaders were convinced it was even more important to make a great show in the conquered and colonized places. Otherwise, people at the fringes of their realm might come under the sway of other influences, tempting them to rebel. So in what was considered backwater Palestine, Roman overlords spared no effort to remind the Jews they were being ruled by the greatest power on earth.

In Jesus' day, Herod Antipas was the governor of Palestine, the regional representative of Tiberias Caesar, the Roman Emperor. Just before Passover each year, Herod would lead a head-of-state procession of military might and extravagant wealth. They marched through the capital city of Jerusalem. Herod stood out from the rest in his resplendent imperial finery. He rode astride a great white stallion, the symbol of victory in war and ultimate rule. His entourage included top generals called "centurions," on their horses, plus a legion of soldiers. At Passover, even the most modest Jewish believers could be whipped up into fervent nationalism, so having an impressive display of Rome's military might would remind them of their tiny place in the global scheme of things.

For centuries throughout the Middle East, horses had been used only by ranking military. They also pulled those deadly chariots, the war tanks of their time. But one year there was a small counterdemonstration that entered Jerusalem through another gate. It started out small.

Actually, it began with a secret plan. When Jesus and the disciples got close to Bethany, just outside of Jerusalem, Jesus told two of his disciples to go into the village. There they would find a colt that had never been ridden before. If someone asked them about taking it, they were supposed to say, "The Lord has need of it." And Mark, the storyteller, adds that they promised to bring it back home immediately afterward. (Mark 11:3)

While the Gospels of Mark and Luke say only that the equine was a colt, Matthew adds important detail. It was a donkey colt, and it came with its mother. Matthew is making an explicit connection that longtime readers of the Jewish Scriptures would understand from the prophet Zechariah: "Lo, your king comes to you; triumphant and victorious is he, humble and riding on a donkey, on a colt, the foal of a donkey." (Zechariah 9:9) This was the promise that a Messiah would come: the one whom God anoints with oil as a sign of his sovereignty, who will finally make all history right, redeeming his people.

For the Jewish citizens crowding around Jesus that day, he was their latest hope to overthrow the Romans. He came among them, not like Herod on a great horse, but riding on a donkey. Donkeys were the beast of burden for the lowest classes, carrying weary travelers and their everyday provisions. Here at last was the fulfillment of the Almighty's promises to the Jewish people! In jubilation, they threw down their cloaks along the roadway. They waved leafy branches symbolizing their praise. They cried out, "Hosanna!" God save us!

It's amazing they didn't all get arrested for this raucous display, but the eyes of the city leaders were fixed on the official procession across town. Ultimately, someone higher up was bound to notice this counterdemonstration. They were not blind to the threat of rebellion.

THEME 2: A Secret Gathering

By Thursday, events were coming to a head, both outside on the streets and for Jesus and his band of disciples.

Throughout the capital city, preparations were being made for Passover, the great celebration of God's liberating the Jews in Egypt centuries ago, when the angel of death struck Egyptian families but "passed over" Jewish homes. That act finally convinced Pharaoh he should let the people called Israel go free. This event became known as the Exodus.

Every year since then, Jews gather around their dinner tables to recite the story of God's gift of freedom. They answer their children's questions about it and eat the symbolic foods that drive its greater meaning deeper into their souls. The Liberator of the Exodus rescued them, offering life, healing, and wholeness. By faith, by adoption into God's family, we Christians join in this celebration of the Exodus, right along with the Jews.

On this particular week, unbeknownst to the crowds outside, Jesus met with his followers, his friends, in a small, upper room. God was about to save *all* people through one human being.

That day has become known as Maundy Thursday. *Maundy* means "commandment," named that because of the "new commandment" Jesus gave to the disciples that evening. "I give you a new commandment," he said, "that you love one another. Just as I have loved you, you also should love one another." (John 13:34)

"God's steadfast love endures forever" is the overriding theme that shines throughout the Hebrew Scriptures. It is a constant reminder of the gracious covenant offered to us by the Ancient of Days. The distinct Hebrew word, *hesed*, means "steadfast love," "covenant loyalty," or "lovingkindness." We can count on the faithfulness of this promise, first given to Abraham, to be our God and to claim us as family. Even Jesus' name affirms this: it means "God saves." Here, on Maundy Thursday, Jesus promised his care for every human being, embodying faithfulness toward us with his very life.

Theme 3: How Could That Friday Be "Good"?

It sounds crazy to call that Friday "good." After Judas' kiss of betrayal on Thursday night in the garden, Jesus was arrested and subjected to an all-night secret trial. Out in the high priest's courtyard, Peter denied his association with Jesus three times. By dawn on Friday, the Jewish high council had accused Jesus of the greatest possible sin: blasphemy. But under Roman law, they could not put a person to death. Only Pilate, the Roman governor, had the power of the death penalty. So the Jewish high council gave Jesus to the Roman guards to deliver to Pontius Pilate.

But once Pilate learned Jesus was from Galilee, he sent the prisoner back to Herod Antipas. There, Herod's soldiers treated Jesus with mockery and contempt. Then Herod returned him back to Pilate for final sentencing. The Books of Matthew and Mark say Pilate wanted to free Jesus for his traditional Passover pardon, but the crowd insisted on his releasing the rebel Barabbas instead. Under pressure from the crowd, Pilate washed his hands of the whole affair and sentenced Jesus to death.

That terrible Friday dragged on. The Roman government believed that nailing convicted criminals to crosses outside the capital cities of their provinces was the most convincing deterrent for future crimes. It took convicts hours, sometimes days, to die from suffocation. Hundreds of crosses routinely stood along the main entryway to Rome. Jerusalem was the capital of its Roman province, so crosses stood on the hill just outside its main gate. Convicts were forced to carry their own crossbars through the city streets to get there. For Jesus, no doubt at the point of exhaustion, the soldiers compelled Simon of Cyrene to carry his crossbar the rest of the way.

The details of Jesus' death are told most fully in Matthew 27:30–44 and Mark 15:22–32. The soldiers gambled for his clothes while he hung dying above them. Ironically coming full circle to Jesus' birth, the placard mockingly nailed to his cross named him as "the king of the Jews." Jesus pardoned one of the two thieves dying next to him. After reciting part of a psalm, Jesus uttered a cry of suffering and victory. Then he breathed his last.

Jesus was betrayed, but he was not an unwitting victim. He intentionally went to Jerusalem to confront his religious antagonists. He *gave* his life for the sins of humanity. Whatever gradations of belief people have had about him since then, Jesus has had a monumental impact on humanity ever since.

To remember God's self-giving love in these terrible events, millions of Christians have recalled the disciples' falling away from Jesus in a worship service called *Tenebrae*. They extinguish one candle as each disciple's name is read. The room finally descends into total darkness without the light of Jesus. A second observance, called "Stations of the Cross," allows worshipers to personally realize something of what Jesus went through on the day he died.

So how could that Friday possibly be "good?" When Jesus gave his life out of love for all people, he expressed the triumph of divine love over death. Good Friday is part of the entire week in which Jesus embodied love for us all. Jesus is the closest, deepest way we can know God's holiness, sovereignty, and love. Even in the midst of the worst of human behavior, we are offered forgiveness and compassion. Jesus' ministry during his physical time on earth, and his willingness to live and die for us, show sheer grace breaking into human history.

We can call that Friday "good" because it demonstrates that nothing we do puts us beyond potential divine forgiveness. Despite human indifference, violence, or betrayal, the Holy One is willing to forgive and to claim us. Are we willing to accept being forgiven?

Questions:

1. How many times have I lost faith in God when my expectations were not met? How would I reconcile celebrating Jesus on Palm Sunday and calling for his death on Good Friday?
2. That Maundy Thursday evening must have brought the disciples together as a close-knit community. Have

I ever participated in a community that felt infused with love and focused deeply on helping others?

3. Have I ever experienced God's forgiveness, knowing I did not deserve it on my own merits? If that has happened, did I keep it to myself, or was I willing to forgive someone who had hurt me?

Things To Do:

1. Light the candle on your dinner table and say:

CANDLELIGHTER: "Jesus shared in the worst of our human experiences,"
ALL AT THE TABLE: "To give us new life and new beginnings."

2. Make a list of Holy Week events outlined in this chapter. Next to each one, note a verse of related Scripture. Then find an object that symbolizes that happening to you. Put each object in a container and number them, so the boxes are in sequence. Over the days of Holy Week, open each container in order, then read the related Bible text. Reflect on the importance of the event and its possible impact on you today.

3. Learn what you can about the Jewish Passover with its symbols and meanings. On Maundy Thursday, host your own version of a Passover *Seder*. You could:
   • Read Exodus chapter 12 (the story of death passing over the Jews and God's leading them to freedom).
   • Next, share a Passover meal using the symbolic foods and their meanings.
   • Then read aloud what Jesus said and did at his last Passover with the disciples. (Mark 14:22–25)

- Finally, offer bread and grace juice (or wine) in Communion remembrance.
4. Imagine yourself interviewing a person in the crowd that week. What would they say just happened? What impact would those events have had on their lives? Some of those you interview might be:

Malchus, whose ear was cut off and healed at Gethsemane (John 18:1–11), or **the man who ran away** from the garden, naked (Mark 14:48–52);

Barabbas, the criminal released when Jesus was condemned (Mark 15:6–15), or **Caiaphas**, the high priest who led the cries for Barabbas' release (Mark 15:11–13);

Pontius Pilate, who ordered Jesus' execution, or **Procula**, his wife, who had a warning dream (Matthew 27:17–19);

Simon of Cyrene, who was made to carry Jesus' crossbar, or **the Roman Centurion** who compelled him to do it (Mark 15:21–22).

The thief who mocked Jesus from his cross, or the **thief who was forgiven** as they were crucified next to Christ (Luke 23:39–43);

Mary, Jesus' grieving mother, or "**the beloved disciple**," who took her into his home (John 19:25–27).

5. If you like to cook or have little helpers in your home, bake something special together. For example, you could let them help you make sugar cookies using a cookie cutter in the shape of a cross. Here is one recipe you might use:

Get the following ingredients: 2 ¾ c. all-purpose flour, 1 tsp. baking soda, ½ tsp. baking powder, 1 c. butter softened, 1 ½ c. white sugar, 1 egg beaten, and ¼ tsp. ground cinnamon (optional).

Find a picture of a cross you want to copy. (There are many types on the Internet.) Save it as a picture, make it the size you want for a cookie and print it out. Trace around it on a piece of paper. Meantime, preheat the oven to 375 degrees F.

Stir the flour, baking soda, and baking powder in a small bowl. Then in a large bowl, beat together the sugar and butter with an electric mixer until it's smooth. Add the egg and vanilla. Gradually blend in the flour mixture.

Roll out the dough into a sheet and cut around your paper cross in the dough to make cross-shaped cookies. Place them 2 inches apart on an ungreased baking sheet. Bake them in the oven for 8 to 10 minutes. Cool them briefly on the baking sheets before putting them on a wire rack to finish cooling.

NINE

The Impossible Happens

———◄o►———

Easter

EASTER—FIFTY DAYS BEGINNING ON EASTER DAY

PETER REFLECTS ON THE STORM:

I WAS SINKING FAST, but for a moment I could see the Teacher from under the water. He reached down to me. I saw his face right over me—amused, almost—and his two strong arms pulled me out of the water. It was like feeling the touch of God.

The wild sea still churned just inches beneath my feet, as he held fast my sodden form. Have you ever been rescued? I was totally relying on him, saved from my own stupidity..

Maybe you've experienced it, too—knowing you are powerless to get out of your situation, and thanking God that the right person is there to lift you up.

Maybe like Mary Magdalene, you get a whole new start—not once but more than you can count in your lifetime. Or like two other Jesus followers, surprised by the Messiah on an ordinary road as they headed home.

———◄o►———

THERE ARE TIMES when words cannot fully convey what is happening. When the impossible occurs, it defies description. That is the Easter event: Jesus' Resurrection, and through him, God's gift of abundant and eternal life to us.

When people around us may be focusing on the Easter bunny, going on egg hunts, and buying "Easter outfits," Christians in their more earnest moments seek to celebrate the greatest Mystery of all: God's touching us personally and redeeming us. The heart of Easter is God's willingness to transform our life now, as well as give us life beyond death. Because Jesus chose to take his love for us all to its final limit, he conquered death as our ultimate fate. Throughout the Easter season, we celebrate the divine Light that breaks into our care-worn world, showing that divine love is stronger than death.

Originally called Eastertide, the Christian season of Easter grew out of the Jewish observance of Passover. It celebrates when God rescued the people Israel from slavery in Egypt long ago, and continues to save people in every generation.

From the second century on, Christians have baptized new believers, symbolically reliving Christ's death and Resurrection. Over the fifty days of Eastertide, they have shared Holy Communion. They have embraced the season as a special time to marvel at Christ's Resurrection: his conquest of death through eternal life. This is why *every* Sunday throughout the Christian Year is considered a "little Easter"—a time to celebrate Jesus' Resurrection from the dead and our dying and rising with Christ.

In the Bible, Paul describes baptism as death and new birth. In Romans 6:3–4, he says we have been buried with Jesus by our baptism into death, so that, just as Jesus was raised from the dead (like Peter was pulled from the water) so that "we too might walk in newness of life." This means we

can live differently, no longer enslaved to the isolation and estrangement that comes from trying to live separate from God.

Easter is about transformation. This is a wonderful message to any of us who may feel we're at the end of our resources or at the end of our hope. We realize once more that our joy is in God. All the old, half-hearted ways of "coping" and "just getting by" can be exchanged for a radically different quality of being.

THEME 1: Double-Crossing Death

Because Jesus conquered death once and for all, our entire year of worship revolves around Easter. Jesus' Resurrection tells us that God's love offers an entirely new life—a new beginning—in every moment. The astounding news of Jesus' life after death is that life can begin again.

No longer is our progression of days simply "marking time" toward death. It becomes an in-depth experience of life in the present and the promise of our eternal life with our God.

The great theologian C.S. Lewis says that in the Christian story, "God descends to re-ascend." God comes "down from the heights of absolute being into time and space, down into humanity." This is the Incarnation, "God With Us," the focus of our worship throughout the Christmas season. Then in the Easter season, we realize more intensely the divine offer of eternal life. Having become human in Jesus Christ, God comes all the way down into human experience to give his life for others. This is how God, in Lewis' words, "[brings] the whole ruined world up with Him."

Lewis compares God's action to a diver who first reduces himself to nakedness, then rushes down into the warm water, then deeper into the black and cold depths with increasing pressure, into the "region of ooze and slime and old decay." Then he surges up again, his lungs almost bursting, back to color and light—until he breaks the surface once again, "holding in his hand the dripping, precious thing that he went down to recover."

You and I are that dripping, precious thing God has recovered. Paul tells this same story by reciting the earliest Christian song in Philippians 2:5–11. He says that Jesus emptied himself of his equality with the Creator, being born in the form of a human being, and more humbly yet, by taking on the estate of the lowest citizen. He was obedient to the point of death on the outrage of a cross. Therefore God has highly exalted Jesus by bringing him back from death. Ultimately, all humanity will bow their knee to him, to the glory of God.

Theme 2: Life in an Unexpected Place

Another insight from Christ's Resurrection is that we can find life even in places where death seems to reign supreme. This is like what happened to Mary Magdalene, who went to Jesus' tomb to privately grieve. (John 20:1–18)

No doubt she wanted to be alone to try to understand the unthinkable events that had taken place after Jesus' arrest. In the wake of the horrific execution she had seen just yesterday, she finally allowed herself to let loose her grief.

To her astonishment, someone had moved the great stone sealing the cave tomb. Peering in, she saw two angels—literally "messengers"—sitting where the corpse should have been. "Woman, why are you weeping?" they asked.

She cried out, "They have taken away my Lord, and I do not know where they have laid him!"

Just then she turned around and saw a gardener. He asked why she was crying and for whom she searched. "Sir," she replied, "if you have carried him away, tell me where you have laid him, and I will take him away."

"Mary." That's all he said. But despite his different form as the Risen Christ, she knew his voice, his inflections, and the fullness of his relationship to her.

"My Teacher!" she rasped, as she rushed to embrace him.

"Do not hold onto me," he said gently, "because I have not yet ascended to the Father. But go to my brothers and tell them, 'I am ascending to my Father and your Father, to my God and your God.'"

So Mary Magdalene ran to the eleven disciples, telling them about her encounter with Jesus. She announced with certainty, "I have seen the Lord!"

Today there are many places we might go to grieve the loss of our loved ones. We may also grieve the loss of so many parts of life, now gone because of the virus and its consequences.

But even in a place of isolation, estrangement or death, we are confronted with the fact of new life. It is not only our physical survival. It's the opportunity to find new meaning and purpose, along with a renewed community perhaps in a different form. In the process, we can recognize the presence and Spirit of the Living Christ.

Mary acted on her new awareness. She confirmed Jesus' real presence, and so gave hope and assurance to those around her.

THEME 3: A Stranger on the Road

The Risen Jesus made four or five appearances we know about after his death (See 1 Corinthians 15:3–8), in addition to others referred to by Paul. Christ made himself known:

- To Peter
- To the eleven disciples (the twelve minus Judas Iscariot, who had committed suicide)
- To "more than five hundred"
- To James, Jesus' brother, who led the Jerusalem Church
- To all the "apostles" (the disciples now called "the sent-out ones") and lastly
- To Paul.

In addition, Mark and Matthew refer to Jesus' being seen in Galilee, and Luke and John write of his appearing in Jerusalem.

Each of these events was a real, totally involving experience that changed the lives of those he encountered. The believers did not recognize his physical appearance because he was in a new form as the Risen Christ. Instead, they identified him by what he did. He spoke to Mary Magdalene in the garden, and gave the disheartened disciples an overabundance of fish, for example. But in one instance two of his disciples saw him in his action of breaking and blessing the bread—that is, in Holy Communion.

Reading Luke 24:13–35, we may be able to imagine the disappointment and despair of those two unnamed followers of Jesus as they walked home on the road to Emmaus after that terrible week of Passover in Jerusalem. In shock after the tragic events that had taken place, they were trying to make sense of it. Then this stranger joined them on the road, appearing out of all the other pilgrims who were making their way back from the capitol to their hometowns.

"What are you discussing while you walk along?" he asked. They stood still, looking sad.

So they told him all about Jesus of Nazareth, and how the chief priests and scribes, their own religious leaders, had delivered him to the Roman governor. And how he had been crucified. "Alas," mourned one, "we had hoped that he was the one to redeem Israel." They added that now, on the third day after his execution, some women were proclaiming they had seen angels, and that he was alive! And that some of his disciples had gone to the tomb and found it empty.

The stranger then spoke. "Was it not necessary that the Messiah should suffer these things and then enter into his glory?"

As they walked, the stranger spoke of Moses and all the prophets, explaining what was told about the Messiah throughout the Hebrew Scriptures.

It was growing dark when these two travelers drew near to their hometown. The stranger acted as if he was going on farther, but they invited him to stay the night. So he agreed. Later, sitting at the supper table, "he took bread, blessed and broke it, and gave it to them. Then their eyes were opened,

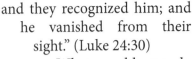

and they recognized him; and he vanished from their sight." (Luke 24:30)

What would you do if this had happened to you? Those two followers turned right around and headed back to Jerusalem. Finding "the eleven and their companions gathered together," they told them what had happened, and how they recognized Jesus at last when he broke the bread.

Communion is not something we do, but *God* does, as a gift of love and grace. When we participate in Communion, we don't just remember "the Last Supper" of Jesus with his disciples. We can also recall his "first breakfast," on the shore of Galilee with seven of the disciples *after* his death and Resurrection. (John 21:1–14)

Yes, Jesus transformed the traditional Hebrew rite of Passover so we would remember him, his teachings, his way of life, and his love. But Communion is also a present experience every time we share it. Just as Jesus did, we ***take, bless, break***, and ***share*** the common elements of food, so it becomes a *Eucharist*: a "thanksgiving" or "thank offering" to God.

As those who want to know Jesus more fully, whenever we share a meal at our own kitchen tables or elsewhere, we follow the same actions Jesus took with those two disciples. We ***take*** the bread, bringing our whole selves before God. Then we ***bless*** the bread, to claim the new covenant which Jesus initiated with his life and death. By doing this, we also claim who we are and to Whom we belong. Next, we ***break*** the bread, to admit the fact of human suffering, not only symbolized in Jesus' broken body, but in all who suffer now for divine justice and compassion. Finally, when we **share** the bread with one another, we share the body of Christ with people who together *are* the body of Christ. Those who share in this supper don't have to be church-goers or religious; they simply try to trust Jesus. That's what the word "faith" means: to trust.

As with Holy Communion, the entire Easter season is a special time to express thanks for what God has done, is doing, and will continue to do to bring us all to the fullness of life.

QUESTIONS:

1. In Matthew 28:10 the Risen Jesus told the women, "Do not be afraid; go and tell my brothers to go to Galilee. There they will see me." Galilee was the place of action and healing during Jesus' ministry, and home territory for many of the disciples. Ask yourself: Where is Galilee for me? Where could I go to share the Good News?

2. What are some of the deathly places in my life or in the world today? Can I see new life or Jesus' presence in some of those seemingly godforsaken places? Are there ways I can help those new beginnings bloom and grow?

3. Who is working today in the Spirit of the Risen Christ to heal the sick, to bring good news to people living in poverty, or to share hope with others? Where do I see the Risen Jesus working in my neighborhood, school, business, or home?

THINGS TO DO:

1. Light the candle on your dinner table and say:

CANDLELIGHTER: "Christ is risen!"
ALL AT THE TABLE: "He is risen indeed!"

2. In many church traditions, the transition from Lent to Easter happens with the lighting of the Paschal (Easter) Candle. You can transfer this tradition to your home. Place a large, white candle in a central location in your home, and light it each evening throughout the fifty days of Easter. If others live with you in your home, invite a different person to light the candle each night, then ask them to say a prayer or to name where they have seen Christ at work around them.

2. Give delight to little ones with decorated eggs. But before you do that, read Luke 24:1–11 about the women discovering Jesus' empty tomb. An egg seems dead but contains new life. It is a Jewish symbol for eternal life. For Christians, the Easter egg is a symbol of the rock tomb out of which Jesus Christ emerged alive.

3. Decide to do something special each week of the Easter season. For example:
   - Make a list of five people for whom you will pray each week. Consider friends, adversaries, and those with whom you'd like to have a better relationship.
   - Write a letter to a person near or far away, expressing your love and appreciation.
   - Celebrate Holy Communion in your own home. Recall Jesus' last supper or his first breakfast with the disciples. Take, bless, break, and share bread, noting the meaning of each

action. If you can do this with others, talk together about where you see God's work in the world. If you live alone, freeze some of the bread to share later with a friend.

- Phone two or three people for a short call to say thank you or to let them know you're thinking of them.
- Give something you have made or value (a plant, an apron, a food, a book) to someone who means a lot to you or whom you want to encourage.
- Pray for your own well-being in the days, weeks and months ahead.

4. You don't have to be a great singer to make music. Look up the words to the "Hallelujah Chorus" from Handel's *Messiah*. Next, choose one of many recordings of it on YouTube or elsewhere. Then turn up the volume and sing along! Remember this is not just for Easter Day; you have the entire fifty-day season.

TEN

A Sudden Calm

Pentecost

Pentecost—Early June to late November

PETER REFLECTS ON THE STORM:

IT ONLY TOOK A SECOND. I shut my eyes for a moment against the swirling mist, and when I opened them again, we were back in the boat. The other guys looked white as a sheet, and I suppose I did, too. But Jesus looked as familiar and as enigmatic as he always did.

It took another moment to realize that the storm had quit! The howling winds were gone. The water was as calm as Galilee under the midday sun, when you could hear the quiet lap of ripples against the sides of the boat. Amazing. The cloud-filled sky was quiet, where just minutes ago it had rained down torrents. Even the wind and waters obey him!

It was a reassuring calm, but at the same time filled with that wild power of the Spirit dancing all around us. I stood stock still, ready to burst with a sense of the divine, overflowing with thanksgiving and joy.

———◇———

JESUS HAD TOLD A JEWISH religious leader that the Holy Spirit is like the wind. As with the wind, we cannot see the Spirit directly, but we can see the evidence of its presence. (John 3:8) Just as we can only see the effects of the wind, it's easiest to see a "before picture" and an "after picture" of the Spirit's effects.

What a difference one day can make! Jesus' followers originally were called *disciples,* meaning "learners." After the outpouring of the Holy Spirit in Jerusalem, they would be called *apostles,* "those who are sent out." Invited to live differently, they engaged in action based on what Jesus had taught and had shown them through his life among them.

One dramatic example was Peter, our now-familiar fisherman. Before Pentecost, he was a rugged, headstrong, impulsive person who had denied his loyalty to Jesus three times. (Matthew 26:69–75) But after the coming of the Holy Spirit, he boldly stood up in front of the international multitude gathered in Jerusalem and told them all about Jesus Christ. No doubt he remained rugged, headstrong, and impulsive, but now he put his life at risk every day because of his devotion to Jesus.

Deriving from the Greek language, the word *Pentecost* means "fifty." Jews mark it as the fiftieth day after Passover, to celebrate the Exodus. (Exodus 14:19–31) It is a special time for them to renew their covenant with the Holy One.

Because of the remarkable events in Acts chapter 2, Christians see this season as an extended time to explore how we can live more fully under the guidance of the Spirit. We seek to recognize the Holy Spirit as the Spirit of the Risen Christ, to embrace the work toward justice and compassion around the globe, and to celebrate the day of Pentecost as the spiritual birthday of the Christian movement around the globe.

So what happened on the day of Pentecost? You can read the story in Acts chapter 2. All of Jesus' disciples had gathered in one place, no doubt hidden away somewhere safe in Jerusalem. They were afraid of being arrested and executed for treason, since their allegiance was to Jesus, not to the Emperor. On that day, the most committed and faithful Jews had come from all over the known world to celebrate Passover in Jerusalem, so it would have been crazy for Jesus' companions to reveal themselves.

Suddenly the sound of a rushing, violent wind filled the place where the disciples were. What looked like "tongues, as of fire" perched above their heads. All of them were filled with the Holy Spirit, giving them the ability to speak in a multitude of world languages.

That must have caused quite a commotion! No longer were they quietly hidden away. The pilgrims outside on the streets could hear their own native languages coming from within. Naturally, a great crowd gathered and wanted to know what was going on. Jesus' followers were all from the small region of Galilee, so how could they know all these languages? "They have to be drunk," growled some naysayers.

To the crowd outside, Peter declared that they were not drunk, because it was only nine o'clock in the morning! Then he told them that Jesus is the Lord, whom God raised up, as foretold in their past by the prophet Joel and by their revered ancestor, King David. Peter concluded (Acts 2:16–36) by saying Jesus is the *Messiah*, the "Anointed One" whom Jews have longed for over the centuries. Jesus has poured out this Spirit, which they were now seeing and hearing firsthand.

Undoubtedly Peter said more than we have been given in Acts about Israel's hopes fulfilled in Jesus Christ. Inspired by Peter's talk—the very first Christian sermon—three thousand people were baptized, devoting themselves to core Christian practices.

THEME 1: A Mighty Wind

In Hebrew the word for "Spirit" also means "breath" and "wind." So this mighty wind blowing over the disciples in Jerusalem must have reminded them of the beginning of their Scriptures, in Genesis chapter 1. It was the beginning of creation, when "a wind from God swept over the face of the waters." (Genesis 1:2) That wind was also the breath of God. This breath/wind is reinforced in the second story of creation, when God formed *adam* (literally meaning "earthling") from *adamah* ("earth") and breathed life into him. (Genesis 2:7) In the disciples' own experience, the Spirit was also the breath of Jesus, after he had died and had risen from the dead. (John 20:25) In that astounding moment, he walked through the locked door and breathed new life on the apostles, saying, "Receive the Holy Spirit."

This is amazing! The Spirit blows across and through our lives: active around, among, and even within us. The Spirit is God moving intimately near us in every time and place. The

Spirit is the Living Christ, present among us, continuing Jesus' ministry. This Holy Spirit of love vivifies every generation.

No single English word adequately captures this dynamic activity of God. The New Testament word for it is *paracletos*, Paraclete: literally, "one who is called in," or "one who comes alongside." The Spirit is the Advocate who pleads our cause as a lawyer would for prisoners before a court. S/He is the Exhorter who rallies us to action. The Gospel of John calls the Holy Spirit "the Spirit of Truth." (John 14:26) John says the Spirit came when the earthly Jesus left us (John 16:7), and continues to live with us as the Risen Christ. (John 14:26) The Spirit is the Witness to Christ (John 15:28) and the fulfillment of Jesus' final promise, "I am with you always, to the end of the age." (Matthew 28:20)

For centuries, a powerful image for the Spirit has been that of fire. John the Baptist had announced Jesus' coming by saying, "He will baptize you with the Holy Spirit and fire." Likewise, when Jesus spoke of his willingness to give his life for us, he said, "I came to bring fire to the earth, and how I wish it were already kindled!" (Luke 12:49)

When we observe the season of Pentecost, we reflect on the Divine Presence active all around us. The Holy Spirit is like an eagle sitting close to us, moving around us, wild and free. We need to be ever alert to God's activity in our midst. The wind and fire of the Spirit can heal and strengthen us to be bold advocates for the work of the Living God.

THEME 2: Global Impact

Just as the Spirit turned Jesus' fearful disciples into bold apostles, so this same Spirit exhorts Jesus' followers today to do Christ's work wherever people are in need. Jesus himself named his mission as the same one the prophet Isaiah had identified centuries before him. (Luke 4:18–21) The Spirit of the Lord is upon me and has anointed me to bring good news to the poor, Jesus said, to proclaim release to captives and recovery of sight to those who are blind, to let the oppressed go free, and to proclaim this year as the year of the Lord's favor, the Year of Jubilee. Then he concluded by announcing, "Today this scripture has been fulfilled in your hearing."

Jesus' proclamation went beyond personal audacity. It implied a direct, personal relationship with God. It also declared the historical "Year of Jubilee," which the ancient Book of Leviticus had announced would take place every fifty years. (Leviticus 25:8–17) A Year of Jubilee would instantly erase all debts and restore all people to their original lands. It would reunite families and "even the playing field" by creating a new beginning for everyone.

When Jesus told his hometown people that this Scripture was now fulfilled, they were shocked and offended. They threatened to throw him off a cliff for blasphemy.

Yet the holy vision of caring for all people persists down through the centuries, both in the Bible and through other religions and philosophies. These days, most likely no one will threaten to throw us off a cliff for doing such things—all except perhaps that Year-of-Jubilee upending of our economy which would cancel out all debts. It is natural for people of different faiths to join with humanitarians of all backgrounds to seek the welfare of *all* people.

In the first Book of the Bible, the story of the Tower of Babel explains the multiplicity of languages as a sign of people being alienated from one another and from God. (Genesis 11:9) But the Day of Pentecost reversed that long-ago action. Jesus' first apostles came from the tiny Galilee region, speaking one dialect. But when the Spirit came upon them, they were able to describe godly deeds of power in every language known at that time. The gift of various languages was a way to share their story of Jesus with the entire world.

It should be no surprise that Scripture read during Pentecost emphasizes how inclusive God's love is toward all human beings. As diverse as we are from one another, we are "all in the same boat" as children of the Holy, Compassionate One. From the Day of Pentecost on, we have been sent out into the world to demonstrate and share this "Good News."

Traditionally, the weeks of Pentecost have been a time to highlight and support Christian ministries around the world. World missions are woven into the fabric of the Bible. From the beginning, Christianity became a global religion, embracing cultural diversity and espousing a more expansive theology. It was rooted in the Middle East, Asia, and North Africa long before it became a European religion.

The Christian missionary movement began early. Howard Culbertson, Emeritus Missions Professor at Southern Nazarene University, estimates that the first Pentecost took place about 30 CE, and four years later persecution prompted Christians to scatter. In 49 CE the Jerusalem Council gave Paul permission to preach to Gentiles (see Acts chapter 15). By 60 CE Paul had completed three full missionary journeys. Culbertson says by the year 200, Christian missionaries had traveled to India, Monaco, Algeria, Sri Lanka, Austria, the Persian Empire, Switzerland, Belgium, and throughout North Africa. Wherever they went, more languages were being added to those first heard in Jerusalem on that initial Day of Pentecost.

THEME 3: The Birthday of the Church

The same awesome wind or breath of the Spirit prompted the apostles the live together differently. From that day on, they devoted themselves to the following core Christian actions:

- Learning about Jesus and faithful living from the apostles' teaching
- Sharing in "fellowship"—*koinonia* (Greek, meaning mutual giving and receiving)
- Breaking bread together—sharing in Holy Communion
- Praying for help in their own situations and for others in need. (Acts 2:42)

In this way the new converts sought to proclaim the Good News of Christ, to embrace new members of the Body of Christ, and to serve the world in the Spirit of Christ. For this reason Pentecost is called "the birthday of the Church."

Listening to the Spirit of Christ is essential for making a faithful, joyful community out of any group. "Where two or three are gathered in my name," Jesus said, "I am there among them." (Matthew 18:20) Unfortunately, the presence of the Risen Christ does not guarantee we will always live with Christian attitudes and caring behavior. Being part of any Christian community is far from perfect. When we worship together, our passion can bring out both the best and the worst in one another. Made up of a broad spectrum of different people because of our diverse gifts, backgrounds and viewpoints, members of any Christian community can experience it as both closer than family and also one's toughest battleground. As writer John Stott says, "Before Christ sent the Church into the world he sent the Spirit into the Church. The same order must be observed today."

Of course the work of Christ's Spirit is not limited to the official Church or exclusive to any single religious institution. The Spirit also expresses God's love through the gift of this Earth, the creatures around us, the witness of Jesus' life, the actions of people, and in countless other ways. God moves among people around the globe, advocates for those being ignored or mistreated, and multiplies caring actions, no matter where or who we are.

QUESTIONS:

1. Who or what is the Holy Spirit to me? Do I see any signs around me that the Spirit is at work? Have I ever experienced the Spirit in my own life?
2. Could humanity's universal language consist of some core life lessons, learned in a variety of different cultures? Are there certain essential messages I think God wants us all to know? If so, what barriers do I need to overcome in order to share those messages through my actions?

3. Can Jesus' followers be "sent out ones" without being part of a community? What kind of a community encourages Christian living at its best? What experiences have I had with Christians, or as a Christian? What do I think is Jesus' relationship to the Church?

Things To Do:

1. Light the candle on your dinner table and say:

CANDLELIGHTER: "The Holy Spirit is alive,"
ALL AT THE TABLE: "working for good within and among us."

2. The Holy Spirit is often seen as the source of passion and creativity. In your own home, you could create six weekly interest centers to explore different dimensions of the Pentecost season. For example:

- Wind—Set up a fan or go outside on a windy day and experience the power of the wind. Look at pictures of trees and clouds in a windstorm. Talk or journal about the wind the disciples must have experienced on the day of Pentecost. Reflect on how the physical properties of the wind and the effects of its power might express our experience of the Holy Spirit.
- Fire—Acts tells us that "divided tongues as of fire appeared among [the apostles], and a tongue rested on each of them." What are some of the mysteries, dangers, and glories of fire? Learn more about different types of fire. If your setting allows it, create a campfire or sit in front of a fireplace and tell stories around it about God at work in the world.

- Multiple languages—On the day of Pentecost, the apostles "began to speak in other languages, as the Spirit gave them ability." What does it take for people not only to speak, but also for those listening to hear what they are saying? Say a couple of sentences in your own native tongue. Then learn the same words in one or two foreign languages.
- Music—Music can help us recapture the elation of those who experienced the Holy Spirit on Pentecost day. It can also help us share joy without the limitations of verbal language. Find some songs about Pentecost, the Spirit, Wind, or the Church. Go ahead, "make a joyful noise!"
- Symbols—You can celebrate God's creative Spirit through your own creativity—by making banners, for example, or designing door hangers for your home. You might cut out felt or paper symbols, such as a star, egg, phoenix, or butterfly, to use as décor. While you are doing this, think about the meaning of each symbol and how it relates to God the Holy Spirit.
- The Church's birthday—Look again at Acts chapter 2 to learn how the Spirit changed the apostles from hiding in a room for fear of persecution and death, and prompted them to go outside and tell others about Jesus. Are there any of the core things those first Christians did that you do, or would like to do more regularly in the future? Make a birthday cake for the Church and share slices with your neighbors. Almost everyone looks forward to a birthday.

3. Make some symbols of the season and give them to neighbors you think might be receptive. You can form the symbols to hang from a mobile, sit on an ornamental branch, or put on a wall banner.

4. If you identify with a particular Christian denomination or movement, research online to see any missions and ministries it may sponsor around the world. Or choose a country or part of the world which intrigues you, then discover what faith-related ministries are occurring in that region. Explore ways you might support a specific effort through your prayers, participation in a micro loan, group hands-on effort, or any other initiative.

5. If you can gather with housemates, family, or friends, talk about the particular gifts each person has. Help one another reclaim the abilities and passions God has given you to enjoy and to share.

Anchoring Each Week

◄○►

Sunday

EVERY SUNDAY

PETER REFLECTS ON THE STORM:

SO WHAT WOULD *YOU* DO if this happened to you? Don't tell me you'd be standing after all of that! We were soaked to the gills, but we just fell to our knees, onto those sloshing floor-boards, and bowed down to him. I'll never forget that moment.

He's not just the Teacher; he's even more. I had hoped for that for a long time, but felt it was too good to be true. Jesus is the Sacred Name in human flesh.

I'm a fisherman. I'm not one to try to figure out all that religion stuff. I just worshiped him. And so did every one of us, each in our own way. It was the right thing to do.

What does it mean to worship, anyway? I think of it as offering our whole selves to the One who made us and who cares for us. Even if we can't be physically gathered with others, we are part of all humanity giving back our wonder and praise.

◄○►

IN NORTH AMERICA, and the United States in particular, the typical work week has expanded to six days a week or more. Especially with smartphones and other electronic devices, bosses and co-workers can expect on-the-job productivity anytime, any day.

So what is Sunday really about? For many people who juggle work and family roles, it has become a mini-mini-vacation, a time to briefly relax between laundry loads and grocery runs for the family. In post-pandemic times, it may be one of the loneliest days of the week, as well.

But Sunday has been—and can be—something altogether different from that.

When I was the Religion Editor for a city newspaper, I covered more than sixty churches, mosques, synagogues, and other spiritual organizations. But a couple of congregational leaders stood out in my mind for their worship-based responses to newspaper topics. One was Barry Beisner, then a rector of the Episcopal church in town, now a bishop. It didn't matter if I was asking about matters of personal faith or community issues for my weekly feature. Whatever the subject, he would naturally tie it to some poetic phrase from his denomination's liturgy: part of a prayer perhaps, or a line from a hymn. Those phrases, like beautiful gems, dotted his seamless sense of identity and connection to God.

I've known one other person like that—the author Madeleine L'Engle, also an Episcopalian. While millions of people know her for her creative science fiction, her nonfiction books are radiant. Writing about her summers spent in upper New York state, she sometimes reflects on her experience of the Holy One, quoting a beautiful phrase from the *Book of Common Prayer*.

I admire those whose worship life seems to seep into their souls, giving them an anchor for living the rest of the week. I'm not good at memorization and don't come from a worship tradition that uses the same repeated prayers. But often a line from a hymn, a phrase, or a sentence will pop out and sit with me for a few days. What's important here is not just a beautifully crafted line of words, but the foundational act of worship itself.

Whatever we consider to be worship, does it give us a rudder by which we can navigate whatever the following week brings to us? Especially when we may not be able to gather easily with others for worship, is there a way to mark Sunday as a special time to honor the presence, word, and action of our Sovereign God?

Yes, as a matter of fact, Jesus' followers have a rich history of worship each week that grounds the other six days. It is one of the most ancient rites of Christianity, begun before 100 CE. Apart from the Seventh Day Adventists who worship on Saturday, all Christians call that day "Sunday." It was the name given by the ancient Romans more than two thousand years ago to worship the sun. But while the planetary name for the day stuck with people down the centuries, the deity faded along with the empire.

Today, Christians know Sunday in three ways.

THEME 1: The Lord's Day

"The Lord" refers to Jesus, whom Christians call "Christ." *Christ* is not a last name; it's Greek for "Lord" or "Master." It is the equivalent of the Old Testament term, *Messiah*, meaning "God's Anointed One." Josephus, one of the first historians, was a Jew of great renown who openly called Jesus "Christ." He also named the new sect "the tribe of Christians."

Sunday worship is not about Jesus Christ—it is not *about* him; it is being *with* him. He is the Risen Christ, alive and present whenever and wherever two or more people gather in his name. (See Matthew 18:20)

One scholar says the Lord's Day is to the other days of the week as yeast is to dough: something strange or foreign that transforms the whole. The Lord's Day has a different rhythm and atmosphere from the rest of the week. It also contains different content—the Communion meal, hosted by Christ himself. Worshipers draw back from the world for a few moments in order to recall God's deep involvement in their everyday lives. That time apart inspires them to return to the world to act on behalf of God's justice and compassion.

THEME 2: The First Day

In Paul's letter to the house church in Corinth, he simply calls Sunday "the first day of the week," which it was on the Jewish calendar, as well. But Sunday is also called The First Day because it reminds people of the first day, or epoch, in the Genesis 1 story: the Creator's establishment of the world.

That creation story names the basic elements of our reality: day and night; the sun, moon, and stars; waters and sky; land and seas; all vegetation; living creatures of every kind; and human beings. In this way Sunday is the anniversary of the creation: all earthly life God has made and continues to sustain. So Sunday prompts people to gratitude and praise by reminding us that the Earth and all that is in it belongs to the Creator. (Psalm 24)

Sunday is also the first day of God's "Word:" the fullness of the Ancient of Days expressed in Jesus himself. This Word was with God from even before Jesus was born. Using poetic language, John 1:1 says, "In the beginning was the Word, and the Word was with God, and the Word was God."

Later in the Bible, the apostle Paul talks about Jesus as the "first fruits" of the *new* creation." He says we will follow Jesus in eternal life after our death. (1 Corinthians 15:20–23) So Sunday is a reminder of Christ's death and Resurrection, and a promise of eternal life for all of us, as well.

THEME 3: The Eighth Day

There is one more big idea about Sunday. While both Jewish and non-Jewish calendars imagined seven days in a week, Christians came to understand Sunday as "the Eighth Day"— the first day of "the eternal day." It stands for time beyond human time: eternal life. The Eighth Day also refers to the

mystery that infuses this life, giving it meaning, purpose, and joy.

The Gospel of John uses a special word for this quality of time: the Greek term *kairos*. It is eternal time that interweaves with normal earthly moments, like interlacing fingers. In these instants, what usually appears to us mortals as a thin veil between earthly life and eternity is swept aside. We live in "abundant life," an eternal quality of living here and now, as well as in life everlasting.

In Jesus' day, Judaism divided history into seven periods. They understood the Jewish Sabbath as "the seventh day," or culmination of creation. So Christians imagined, in the end times, a new age which would never end, which they called "the Eighth Day." By using this phrase, early Christians meant the beginning of a new world. They remembered the first Eighth Day, when the disciples saw the empty tomb and realized that Jesus had risen from the dead.

This does not mean that people who go to church on Sunday think they have been to heaven and back. But if they have experienced a sense of the Living Christ in some word of Scripture, in a hint of music or internally in prayer, they may feel they have glimpsed something, Someone, who is real beyond all of our human trials and endless preoccupations.

QUESTIONS:

1. Are there relationships in my life that point to something larger than just daily concerns or my detailed

schedule? Have I ever felt a mystery beyond what I can see and prove?

2. What, if anything, prompts me to pray? Have I ever sensed the presence of Someone more than myself in moments of awe, joy, or sorrow? If so, at such times, what was I prompted to think, say, or do?

3. How can I celebrate any Sunday—maybe every Sunday—as "the first day:" a reminder of all life around me and within me? What might I do, by myself or with close friends, to embrace the idea of abundant life even beyond this lifetime?

THINGS TO DO:

1. Most people don't live in a waking world of "lords" and "ladies," so the term "Lord" or "Lady" might not have much meaning for you. How could you show honor to God with your language? And in your relationships? Think about people whose way of living has honored the Giver of Life. If they are people you know, send a card or write them a thank you note. Look up online or follow-up with friends to rediscover those you might have lost touch with along the way.

2. Draw or paint a picture, or engage in a physical posture to honor God.

3. Allow some part of each Sunday to experience God's creation. Find a place to be in nature and explore the intricacy of creation. Go for a walk in a wild place near you. Take some photographs or make some sketches of what inspires you.

4. Learn about some forms of spirituality that are new to you, perhaps using Adele Ahlberg Calhoun's *Spiritual Disciplines Handbook: Practices That Transform Us.* It is an excellent, comprehensive guide.

5. Plan activities that express thanks for the world God has made and show good stewardship of it. For example:
    - Get personally involved in an activity to celebrate Earth Day in April. Clean some part of your community
    - Read Psalm 24 aloud, then write a poem about one of the creatures mentioned in it
    - Learn about an endangered species and someone who is doing something to save it
    - Say a prayer that blesses the animals around you
5. Reflect on how the things you do on Sunday are or can be different from what you do the other days of the week. Set up a place in your home for a few moments of devotions or journaling. Make an effort to come to that place each Sunday to pray, sing, or do some inspirational reading.

The Gift of Each Day

Canonical Hours

EVERY DAY

PETER REFLECTS ON THE STORM:

HE WAS AS SOAKED as we were, and wearing that familiar grin. He hardly looked glorious. I might have laughed out loud in other circumstances, except for what he had just done.

"Truly, you are the Son of God!" Still on our knees, we stumbled over the words.

I had heard the words used by the Romans, but they came from those who worshiped Caesar. "Son of God" meant a person who represented here on Earth the supposed god he served. But huddled in our leaky boat, we realized *Jesus* is the unique Son of the true God! In Jesus, the Author of our lives chose to live among us as one of us. Jesus will rule God's people through to the end times. Those fancy religious leaders can call it blasphemy if they want. But we knew it for a fact.

So now—*after* we realize who he is and worship him— how do we stay anchored in him, wherever we are, whatever we are doing?

WHEN THE HOLIDAYS are over, most people I know would go back to what they considered normal. They return to filling up their schedules, focusing on their jobs or on their children, or both. All of this can be good! But after the first onset of this latest virus, none of that may be "normal" anymore, at least in the same way. Going out of the house for more than essential errands may not be so rare anymore, but can still be dangerous to the health of the youngest and oldest members of the household or the medically fragile.

And then there's the "ordinariness" that can set in, whatever our freedoms and limitations. But what if we made every day a reminder of who we are and of the One to whom we belong? This is not a generic question, but a specific one: *every* day.

THEME #1: One Hour at a Time

Years ago, I volunteered for a month with the Ecumenical Institute. The leaders introduced me to something called the Daily Offices, or "Canonical Hours." These Hours are such an ancient tradition that, except for people in Religious Orders—Benedictines, Jesuits and other Religious Orders living in convents and monasteries—most Christians are unaware of the practice altogether.

Observing the Canonical Hours is a way of living every twenty-four-hour period by marking specific times in Jesus' life and ministry, and recalling particular themes of Christian living. Benedict (c. 480–c. 547), founder of the Benedictine Order, set the basis for this pattern of daily prayer in his Rule for Monasteries. Over the years, minor differences in the Canonical Hours developed in the various monastic traditions. So in the 1970s, the Ecumenical Institute divided each day neatly into three-hour increments. The adapted Hours are:

Vespers .... From 6 to 9 p.m.
Compline .... From 9 p.m. to midnight
Matins .... From midnight to 3 a.m.
Lauds .... From 3 a.m. to 6 a.m.
Prime .... From 6 a.m. to 9 a.m.
Terce .... From 9 a.m. to noon
Sext .... From noon to 3 p.m.
None .... From 3 p.m. to 6 p.m.

Each twenty-four-hour day begins in the evening, following the Jewish tradition.

Those who practice Canonical Hours participate in a brief worship sometime within each time period. To follow a printed week of Canonical Hours, you can get the small book, *The Divine Hours Pocket Edition* by Phyllis Tickle. Or you can simply reflect on the Bible text for each Hour listed in this book, then read part of the related psalm, or say the prayer. Trying such a pattern a few times might develop into a natural rhythm, enhancing your awareness of God as the anchor for your daily living.

Theme #2: The Dark Hours

Vespers, 6 to 9 p.m.

Some people may be familiar with the term "Vespers" because of a tradition in their school, church, or residential community, where a person leads a brief worship service at about dinnertime. Since the focus for Vespers is on Jesus at the Last Supper, any evening meal could inspire us to express our gratitude, giving thanks for the gifts we have received through the events of the day. Prayer at this time could be either spontaneous or planned. There are no specified words. Here are three options for what you might do:

- Focus for meditation: Jesus at the Last Supper (Matthew 26:26–28)
- Reading a Psalm: Psalm 100 (Worship and sing to God)
- Possible prayer:
  Ancient of Days, I thank You for the day now past: for those things accomplished and even for what remains undone. Help me not to be anxious about superficial things, but to clasp tight to that which endures. I pray for a greater faith and a deeper trust in You, so I will live how You have called me to be. This I pray in the name and the way of Jesus Christ. Amen.

Compline, 9 p.m. to midnight

The Bible shows how God has been faithful to the divine covenant with us, from the time of Abraham on. This vow was to be our God and to claim us as God's family. But this same history also reveals how often we have fallen short on our side of the relationship. For example, when Jesus was in his hour of greatest need, in the garden of Gethsemane, his disciples faltered in their prayers for him and succumbed to sleep. (Matthew 26:30ff.) So the Hour of Compline is a time of penitence, as we examine our conscience and each day's events.

- Focus for meditation: The Garden of Gethsemane (Matthew 26:30–46)
- Reading a Psalm: Psalm 25:4–10 (Help me when I'm suffering)
- Possible prayer:
  You have redeemed me, oh God, from all my wandering ways. I confess I have not been consistent in living my life completely for You, no matter how much I try. I want to learn from Your teachings, reflect them in all my relationships, and rest in Your love. I place my spirit into Your hands. This I pray in the name and the way of Jesus Christ. Amen.

MATINS, MIDNIGHT TO 3 A.M.

The middle of the night can be a good time to reflect on the big picture of our lives. Over the centuries many Christians have pondered the promise of Jesus' "Second Coming," when the Holy One will send Christ to judge our living in the context of justice and mercy. That time is not intended to elicit our fear, but rather humility and gratitude for God's compassion. No doubt it will also be a time of wonder, since we're told it will come with creation's fulfillment. Matins is a time of watchful waiting, reflecting on Christ's final coming.

- Focus for meditation: The ten young women (Matthew 25:1–13)
- Reading a Psalm: Psalm 27:1,11–14 (Wait with courage)
- Possible prayer:

Light of all life, I thank You for all that lies ahead in this new day, and for the gift of Your living presence in every moment. Guide me in my waking to watch for Christ, and guard me in my sleeping, to rest in Your peace. Help me to be ready when Christ comes again. This I pray in the name and the way of Jesus Christ. Amen.

LAUDS, 3 TO 6 A.M.

Lauds (pronounced to rhyme with "odds") is a time to celebrate Jesus' Resurrection. When the women went to Jesus' tomb as soon as the Jewish Sabbath was over, they expected to put spices on his corpse to complete his burial. But the tomb was empty! He was no longer dead. He had gone ahead of them back to Galilee. (Matthew 28:1–10) The Bible tells us his new life conquered death forever, so death is no longer our final end, either. (Romans 6:3–4)

- Focus for meditation: Discovering the empty tomb (Matthew 28:1–9)
- Reading a Psalm: Psalm 150 (Praise God everywhere in every way)
- Possible prayer:

God of Jesus Christ, my soul exults in You! I thank You for the beauty and variety of Your creation, and for Your gift of new creation offered to us all. I rejoice in Christ's Resurrection and through him, Your gift of eternal life. Help me live my life as a new creature by Your grace. This I pray in the name and the way of Jesus Christ. Amen.

THEME #3: The Light Hours

PRIME, 6 TO 9 A.M.

What we do speaks louder than our words and expresses most powerfully what we believe. After Jesus had been teaching the disciples, letting them get to know him and see him in action, he sent them out to act on what they had witnessed. He passed on to them his own mission: to bring good news to the poor, to proclaim release to those who are captive, to bring recovery of sight to the blind, and to let the oppressed go free. (Luke 4:18)

The Hour of Prime helps us prepare for whatever work or activity may lie ahead in each day. Even the humblest task can be done in love. Prime reminds us of God's personal call to engagement, giving us the opportunity to dedicate ourselves anew. Whatever we do, we can "be doers of the Word and not hearers only." (James 1:22)

- Focus for meditation: The doers (Matthew 28:19–20)
- Reading a Psalm: Psalm 147:1–6 (God heals and gathers the outcasts)
- Possible prayer:
  Our merciful God, You have brought me safely into this day. I thank You for all those who have gone before me, acting on Your Good News. I praise You for Your Son and dedicate this day's activities to You. Give me the grace to be obedient to Your goodness, declaring Your Word by what I do. This I pray in the name and the way of Jesus Christ. Amen.

Terce, 9 a.m. to noon

Whether our engagement is physical, mental or emotional, for many of us by mid-morning our work calls for commitment. Especially in times of trouble, we realize we are totally dependent on our Divine Advocate to get us through the demands of the day. Terce reminds us to ask for God's help to accept the palpable presence of the Holy Spirit. The Spirit comes with energy and purpose that can surprise us as well as others, extending our reach far beyond expected boundaries.

- Focus for meditation: The Holy Spirit at Pentecost (Acts 2:1–21)
- Reading a Psalm: Psalm 67 (May God's way be known everywhere)
- Possible prayer:

Mighty Wind and Breath of Life, I depend upon You. Human beings are frail creatures. We rely on Your mercy and compassion to be able to stand as Your people. You sustain my life, so I trust in You and choose not to be afraid. Please come as the Holy Spirit to help make me worthy of what You call me to do. This I pray in the name and the way of Jesus Christ. Amen.

SEXT, NOON TO 3 P.M.

These are the midday hours in which Jesus gave his life for us. It's a time to ask for help from the Living God and to join in Christ's victory over death. In the face of suffering and loss, we can recall Paul's soaring words beginning with "If God is for us, who is against us? . . . [Nothing] in all creation will be able to separate us from the love of God in Christ Jesus, our Lord." (Romans 8:31,39)

At this Hour, we may remember the pain and isolation of so many people around us and of those who have died. Even in extreme situations, God is the source of our ability to withstand trials and make faithful decisions.

- Focus for meditation: Christ on the cross (Matthew 27:45–54)
- Reading a Psalm: Psalm 118:21–24 (The rejected stone is our cornerstone)
- Possible prayer:

Oh You who has chosen to dwell among us, I pray that You will give us a compelling social vision, that new forms of human care will become a living reality. In this moment, I dare to humbly say along with Jesus Christ, "Into Your hands I commend my spirit." Please guide and empower me to live that assertion throughout this day. I pray these words in the name and the way of Jesus Christ. Amen.

None, 3 to 6 p.m.

Midafternoon is often a time that calls for "steadfast perseverance," undergirding ourselves for the rest of the day. None (rhymes with "own") is also an excellent time to strengthen ourselves for the end of this earthly life. We can reaffirm that as Jesus Christ has triumphed over death, he now reigns forever. Whether in this life or the next, we can declare with the psalmist, "I shall live for God!" (Psalm 22:29)

- Focus for meditation: The Throne (Matthew 25:31–46)
- Reading a Psalm: Psalm 22:29–31 (I choose to live for the Deliverer of the living and the dead)
- Possible prayer:

Lover of our souls, You have created us for relationship. I confess how often I would prefer to live out of the past rather than risk creating new ways of relating to others. Push me to turn to face the future on behalf of all people, as You have done through Your Son. Help me focus my life, I pray, so that when Christ comes again I will freely join with all the angels in praising You. I pray this now in the name and the way of Jesus Christ. Amen.

The point of these hourly practices is not to mimic some old-time ritual, but to recall Jesus' work among us and to find our bearings through God's presence and purpose. The Canonical Hours remind us that every day is a precious gift, and every hour is an unrepeatable opportunity to receive and to show the One who reigns in love.

QUESTIONS:

1. Are there any worship practices I have done frequently? What have been my experiences with prayer or other times when I was aware of God's presence? Have any of those experiences helped me get through difficult times?

2. What has been my usual pattern as I've come to the evening and night hours? What themes from the "Dark Hours" (Vespers, Compline, Matins, or Lauds) might help me gain a more complete perspective on life or on my relationship with God?

3. How could the way I start my day be inspired or strengthened by doing something from any of the "Light Hours" (Prime, Terce, Sext, or None)? Are there any of those practices I might want to try? How might I use or adapt them in my unique situation?

THINGS TO DO:

1. If you wake up in the night and have trouble getting back to sleep, try doing a brief worship for that time in the Canonical Hours. It may remind you of God's care for you and give you a sense of peace.

2. Choose a time in Jesus' life from a Canonical Hour and focus on it. Read about the event in the Bible, then draw or paint a picture to represent that situation. Reflect on its importance to you in a meditation. Pick one of the Hours' spiritual themes and write a poem

or journal about how it speaks to you. If this practice helps you, consider doing it more often.

3. Find a safe, private place to experiment with having a brief worship in a daylight Canonical Hour. If this feels strange at first, that's normal. Give it time; dwell in it. Even if it gives you only a small comfort, you may want to try it again another day.

4. If you have found that some short service of Canonical Hours works well for you, consider doing it as part of a retreat day when you're exploring the outdoors in solitude or with friends. Try turning these experiences into journaling or artwork—whatever expresses you best.

Coming Full Circle

Having the Time of My Life

ALL THE TIME

After times of tumult as in the wake of a pandemic, many of our social anchors still feel uncertain. What of these is worth risking now? At the same time, damage has been done by disagreements over basic "facts" about health issues. For many people, those arguments have turned health decisions into a divisive political war zone. The roiling waters can make us feel lost at sea once more. Given how quickly long-standing traditions and a sense of community can fall away, the enduring

Christian worship seasons can offer us permanent, reassuring shores.

Our times are and always have been in God's hands, not ours. Regardless of past imagined comforts and conveniences, we have never known God's plans for our present or for our future. As with Jesus' disciple Peter in the midst of that Galilean storm, it all comes down to faith—which means *trust*.

Trust in God does not mean passivity. Sometimes it involves boldly risking, or actively waiting, or creating community—all while living courageously in each present moment. In both ordinary and extraordinary times, it is not for us to know ultimate purposes. We are to keep alert, to pray at all times guided by the Spirit, (Ephesians 6:18; 1 Thessalonians 5:17; Jude 1:20) and to make known the mystery of Christ's presence among us all. (Colossians 1:25–26)

So after the storm of a pandemic or at any other period of stress and trauma, we can connect to the recurring seasons of Christian worship to find our bearings in time once more. The awareness of God's presence offers us a deeper appreciation of sacred time interlaced with our daily activities, as we come to view these days with new eyes. It teaches us to know Jesus better, realizing deep connections to one another in a vibrant life that is offered to us all.

As Jesus invited Peter, he may invite us to "get out of the boat:" to experience seemingly impossible events, even in the midst of life's most daunting storms.

Whatever our background or personal convictions, God has made us all part of the family. We can respond out of our deepest human impulse—to worship the One who created us, who sustains and saves us. Jesus shows us that despair and death are not our final end. Whatever the circumstances, we can seek to steer our lives in line with God's grace. We can celebrate a different calendar. The circle of seasons reminds us of God's movement among us, leading us to a new shore.

"Now may the Lord of peace himself give you peace
at all times
in all ways. The Lord be with all of you."
(2 Thessalonians 3:16)

Chapter Endnotes

Chapter 2: Lost at Sea

1. "Global boiling: An ominous warning," p. 17 of the August 11, 2023 issue of *The Week*. The curated article cited Jack Healy in *The New York Times*, Madison Pauly in *Mother Jones*, Dr. Leana Wen in *The Washington Post*, and Scott Simon in *NPR.com*.

2. *The Social Dilemma*, 2020 Netflix film documentary, on the impact of social media. Link: https://www.google.com/search?q=The+Social+Dilemma%2C+2020+Netflix+film+documentary&sxsrf=APwXEdd0k788UU2hp94s-figEikRO1oAmlQ%3A1687874889500&source=hp&ei=Se2aZKe-HP31k PIPy4CziA8&iflsig=AOEireoAAAAAZJr7WZ_5AwE9g0D cteb6ROZHMwPc2KrD&ved=0ahUKEwjnhtn5z-P_ AhX9OkQIHUvADPEQ4dUDCAo&uact=5&oq= The+Social+Dilemma%2C+2020+Netflix+film+ documentary&gslcp=Cgdnd3Mtd2l6EAMyBQghEKs CUABYAGC4OWgBcAB4AIABbogBbpIBAzAuMZgBA KABAqABAQ&sclient=gws-wiz

Chapter 3: The Christian Year— Finding Our Bearings

1. Ireton, Kimberlee Conway. *The Circle of Seasons: Meeting God in the Church Year*, p. 14.

Chapter 6: Epiphany—Looking Forward

1. You can hear Paul Harvey's telling of this story on YouTube at: https://www.youtube.com/watch?v=EcjuK5KUe4M

Appendix

"Worship Arts Through the Christian Year"

A GUIDE FOR WORSHIP USING THE ARTS AND THE WORD TO ENHANCE THE CHRISTIAN SEASONS

BY CAROL S. KERN

THIS WORKSHOP is a fun, interactive way to help your community directly experience the Christian Year. Participants walk through learning centers, using their senses to reflect more deeply on the meaning of each season. The two-hour walk-through provides an opportunity for people to smell, taste, touch and see things that engage them in a deeper experience of the seasonal themes.

The process of making the six "seasons" can be an enjoyable learning adventure, as well. Open, upended refrigerator boxes provide the structure for each center. They are then painted the color of the season and is "dressed" with one or more related banners, a phrase or question to ponder, and three-dimensional objects for the visitors to use. When two or more people create the centers together, listening to each other's ideas and incorporating them adds to the experience. Be sure to take pictures of the final stations. They will spark more creative ideas for the next time you do the workshop.

A PRACTICAL WALK THROUGH
THE CHRISTIAN YEAR

This "hands-on" stroll through the seasons of the Christian Year includes special emphasis on Lectionary readings from the Bible, experiences designed to touch each one of the senses, and creative activities the participants can take home.

It is intended for people who are designing and leading worship, for Sunday school leaders, artists, and musicians, and all those interested in bringing worship to life in their church. It also could be a great learning experience for children and youth in Home School or attending Christian schools.

Each worship season learning center is defined by a large refrigerator box painted and decorated to match the particular season. Participants gather as a small group within these learning centers and walk their way through the year, season by season at intervals of fifteen minutes to a half hour each, according to the leader's plan. Arriving at each learning center, the group follows the outline of activities to do on the handout. If the class is small, all participants may move as one group together through the seasons.

Handouts could include:

* A set of directions for moving through the seasons
* A chart for each half of the Christian Year (See The Christmas Cycle and The Easter Cycle which follow here)
* An article about the Three-Year Common Lectionary

A copy of this book, *Tossed in Time*, is an important background resource for each participant.

THE CHRISTMAS CYCLE

Advent	Christmas	Epiphany
	WHEN	
4th Sunday before Christmas Eve.	December 25 to January 5.	January 6 to Ash Wednesday, the first day of Lent.
	HISTORY	
In the 4th century early Christians saw need for a preparatory time before Christmas, as Lent was before Easter.	4th century Christians wanted to celebrate specific events in Jesus' life. December 25 was first mentioned around 354 CE. Christmas celebrations in Rome took the place of pagan winter festival.	Came out of the Eastern churches as a festival of the birth and baptism of Jesus. The Western Church celebrated his birth at Christmas. and the Magi coming at Epiphany.
	MEANING	
"Coming" birth of Christ. Ancient meaning: The second coming of Christ to judge us all.	"Christ's Mass" (Old English).	"Manifestation" of God in Jesus Christ.
	THEMES	
Expectation of birth Preparation: spiritual Christ is still coming to judge by grace. Anticipation Redemption.	The Word become flesh. Light: Jesus is the light of the world conquering darkness.	Journey of Magi / star Life and ministry of Jesus: baptism, miracles at Cana, call of disciples, healing the sick, transfiguration.
	COLOR	
Purple for majesty. Blue for hope and for Mary, mother of Jesus.	White and gold—festive celebration colors. White for purity.	Green for growth.
	TIME	
About 4 weeks	Twelve days.	Four or more weeks, depending on placement of Easter.
	RESOURCE	
Pages 196–216 in United Methodist Hymnal	Pages 217–251 in United Methodist Hymnal	Pages 252–67 in United Methodist Hymnal

THE EASTER CYCLE

Advent	Christmas	Epiphany
WHEN		
40 days before Easter. Does not include Sundays ("little Easters").*	Sunday after the first full moon on or after the first Day of spring. Can be anytime from March 22 to April 25.	50th day after Easter. Ascension is 40 days after Easter Day.
HISTORY		
Linked with Easter and a A time to prepare for a special day of baptism in the early church. Later and the theme changes to penitence and mourning for sin, connected to Jesus' 40 days in the wilderness. By 5th century it was preparation for all Christians for Easter renewal.	Grew out of the Jewish Passover celebration, Pasha. Second century Christians used it as a time for baptism followed by Holy Communion.	Linked at first with the Jewish celebration of First Fruits of Harvest. Later Christians tied Pentecost the Holy Spirit's birth of the Church to the gift of the Torah (Ten commandments) on Mt. Sinai.
MEANING		
Preparation.	Resurrection of Jesus Christ. Promise of abundant and eternal life. Took name from Eastre, pagan goddess of spring.	"Fiftieth" in Greek, for 50 days after Easter. Coming of the Holy Spirit.
THEMES		
Penitence before renewal. Temptation Jesus in the wilderness. Sin, suffering, passion. Lord's Last Supper. Fasting, sorrow.	Resurrection—Risen Christ. Creation of the Earth New creation. The cross and the empty tomb.	Dove of peace. The Holy Spirit: fire, flames, wind, breath. The Church's birthday.
COLOR		
Purple or violet for penitence and passion. Black on Good Friday.	White, gold, and silver for festive celebration.	Red for fire. Green for "ordinary time" = days put in order.
TIME		
From Ash Wednesday to Easter eve—46* days.	From Easter Day until Pentecost—50 days.	One day, then ordinary time up to beginning of Advent.
RESOURCE		
Pages 278–301 in United Methodist Hymnal.	Pages 302–27 in United Methodist Hymnal.	Pages 328–336; 537–544 in United Methodist Hymnal.

Seasons and Rhythms of the Church Year: Learning Centers

You can design the refrigerator-box learning centers using two or three of the following ideas to invite the participants to personally engage.

THE CHRISTMAS CYCLE:
ADVENT—CHRISTMAS—EPIPHANY

ADVENT: Four weeks before December 25

1. As you enter the seasonal worship space think about the symbolic color, its meaning, and its impact on you at first glance. Discuss this with the others.
2. Choose a set of Scriptures on one of this year's cards for one of the four Sundays in Advent [from the Three-Year Common Lectionary] and light an Advent candle for that Sunday.
3. Draw and cut out symbols from the scripture theme and attach it to the purple wall.
4. Add words to the wall that express human need in this time of preparation for Jesus' coming.

5. Sing an Advent song, such as "O Come, O Come, Emmanuel;" "Come, Thou Long-Expected Jesus;" or "Toda la Tierra."

CHRISTMAS: December 25 through January 5

1. As a group, choose and sing a favorite Christmas carol.
2. Have one person read Luke 2:1–20. Then light the Christmas candle.
3. Think about your favorite Christmas story. If you are able, share this story with someone in your group.
4. What do you think it means when people refer to Jesus as "the Word made flesh?"
5. Dance to the Christmas carol "Angels We Have Heard on High."

EPIPHANY: January 6 for 40 days plus Sundays

1. Read Matthew 2:1–12 about the visit of the wise men. Imagine their long journey to see Jesus, and their decision not to tell Herod where the child was.
2. If you have some frankincense in the worship center, light the incense and smell its fragrance. Talk about how the meaning of the wise ones' gifts might have said something important about Jesus' future adult life.
3. Read Isaiah 9:1–4. What difference does it make to have a Messiah "in the flesh" rather than just one spoken about in Old Testament prophesies?
4. How can the theme of "light" be used throughout this season in your church or in your family?

THE EASTER CYCLE:
LENT—EASTER—PENTECOST

LENT: Ash Wednesday until Easter Eve

1. Discuss the meaning of the symbols and colors for Lent.
2. Read aloud Matthew 4:1–11. What is a temptation you need to face at this time? Write it on a card and place it at the base of the cross. (No one else will read these cards.)
3. If you painted "Wrestling with Decisions" on the Lent worship center, ask each person to write down an important decision you have to make. Silently ask for God's help to make that decision.
4. Get ready to share in a meal to remember of Christ's last supper and his undying love for us.

EASTER: Fifty days beginning on Easter Day

1. Read John 20:1–18 like a radio drama. Assign parts as you find the characters and add a narrator.
2. Share some Easter reflections and stories about how you have experienced Easter.
3. Read 1 Peter 1:3–9 and talk about how Jesus' Resurrection gives you "a living hope" or joy.
4. Sit back and enjoy listening to Handel's "Hallelujah Chorus."

PENTECOST: Early June to late November

1. Read aloud Acts 2:1–21 and recall what happened that day.

2. View the scene from *Forrest Gump* where the feather floats on the wind. Think about what this might show about the Holy Spirit.
3. If you have a basin of water, ask someone in the group to read 1 Corinthians 12:3–13. Feel the water and remember your baptism.
4. Sing Happy Birthday to the Church, blow out the candles, and have a piece of cake.

Seasons to Celebrate—Leader's Notes

The following are notes to help you lead the "Worship Arts Through the Christian Year" workshop. It is described in this book's chapter on Finding Our Bearings. The rest of this appendix gives you details on how to create the worship season learning centers.

ADVENT—PREPARE THE WAY
Four weeks before December 25

Music—Godspell and Taizé. "Prepare the Way of the Lord." "O Come, O Come Emmanuel."

Visuals—Blue [or purple] background. Two fabric panels deal with the first two scriptures below. Advent banner of the four Advent candles. Banner proclaiming "Make straight in the desert a highway for our God." Four Advent candles: three blue [or purple], one rose.

Scripture—

Isaiah 2:1–5   Let us go to the mountain of the Lord
Matthew 24:36–44 You must be ready for His coming
Isaiah 11:1–10   Root of Jesse. Peaceful kingdom
Matthew 1:18–25   Angel appears to Joseph. Emmanuel.

The Flow—
1. Explanation of the colors, visuals, Advent candles and music
2. Give each person in the group a part: four scripture readers, one candle lighter.
3. Play the first part of *Godspell's* "Prepare the Way of the Lord" and move from it to the Taizé chant. {Or other music]
4. Read Isaiah 2:1–5. Light the first candle. Sing verse 1 of "O Come, O Come, Emmanuel."
5. Read Isaiah 11:1–10. Light the second candle. Sing verse 4 of "O Come, O Come, Emmanuel."

6. Read Isaiah 7:10–16. Light the rose candle. Sing verse 5 of "O Come, O Come, Emmanuel."
7. Read Matthew 1:18–25. Light the fourth candle. Sing verse 7 of "O Come, O Come, Emmanuel."
8. Discussion: The human needs for a Messiah have changed through the last 2,000 years. What are the present world's needs?
9. Sing with guitar, "Toda la Tierra."

CHRISTMAS—WORD MADE FLESH
December 25 through January 5

Music—A recording of "Angels We Have Heard on High" plus your denomination's hymnal

Visuals—White background. JOY banner. White Christmas Candle. Video of stable and sheep.

Scripture—

Luke 2:13,14	Angels sing "Glory to God"
Hebrews 1:1–4	Jesus is God's Son, bearing God's imprint

The Flow—
1. Ask persons to read the two scriptures and one to light the candle.
2. Gather all so they can see the monitor. Show the video of the stable. Play "O Come, All Ye Faithful" while it is being shown.
3. Lead a discussion on "Is something wrong here?"
4. Read Luke 2:1–20. Light the white Christ Candle.
5. Dance the Christmas carol, "Angels We Have Heard on High."
6. Read Hebrews 1:1–4.
7. Sing some favorite Christmas carols, either from the hymnal or spontaneously.
8. Share some Christmas stories.

EPIPHANY—FROM DARKNESS TO LIGHT
JANUARY 6 FOR 40 DAYS PLUS SUNDAYS

Music—Recorded music for background during time of remembering your baptism.

Visuals—Green background. Bowl of water with small stones (for people to keep). Three king crowns. Gold, frankincense, and myrrh.

Scripture—

Matthew 2:1–12	The Magi or three kings
Matthew 3:13–17	Baptism of Jesus
Isaiah 9:1–4	Those who sat in darkness have seen a great light

The Flow—

1. Talk about the colors, scripture themes, and the gifts of the Magi.
2. Ask persons to read the scriptures and play the parts of the three kings.
3. Read Matthew 2:1–12.
4. Present the drama from *A Season to Celebrate* "The Three Kings" by Allen Pote.
5. Read Matthew 3:13–17 about the baptism of Jesus.
6. Invite those who wish to remember their baptism: come to the bowl, feel the water, and take a stone home to continue the memory of this event. Play music in the background.
7. Read Isaiah 9:1–4, "Those who sat in darkness have seen a great light."
8. Lead a discussion: What difference does it make to have a Messiah "in the flesh" rather than just one spoken about in Old Testament prophesies?

LENT—WRESTLING WITH TEMPTATIONS— FACING TOWARD JERUSALEM
Ash Wednesday until Easter Eve

Music—Background music while people come to the cross and share the Love Feast / *Agape* meal: "Lily and the Lamb" by the Anonymous Four.

Visuals—Purple background, small wooden cross, black drape, palm branch, cup and plate. Pitcher and towel, "Watch and pray" banner. Communion banner. Large wooden cross to place on the floor or on a low table.

Scripture—

Matthew 4:1-11   Temptation of Jesus
Matthew 21:1-11   "Passion" of Jesus: his suffering and death

The Flow—

1. Discuss the meaning of the various colors and visuals.
2. Choose two people to read the scriptures, two to help with the hand washing, one to pass out index cards and pencils, and one to hand out palm branches.
3. Read Matthew 4:1-11 (the temptation of Jesus).
4. Ask the question, "What is a temptation that you must face at this time? Write it on a card and put it at the foot of the cross."
5. Read Matthew 21:1-11 (Jesus' suffering and death). Hand out palm branches.
6. Invite all to come up and wash their hands to prepare for sharing an "*agape* meal" or Love Feast of grape juice and bread. The purpose of the meal is to remember Christ's

undying love for us and our love for him and for one another as his people. Then share in the meal.

7. When all have received and have eaten the food, allow a couple of minutes for silent prayer.
8. Start singing "Were You There?" Invite all to join in.

EASTER—LIVING HOPE
FIFTY DAYS BEGINNING ON EASTER DAY

Music—A recording of Handel's "Hallelujah Chorus."
Visuals—Colorful drape. White candle. White background. Butterfly.
Scripture—

1 Peter 1:3–9	Jesus' Resurrection gives us a living hope and inheritance
John 20:19–31	Christ appears to disciples and to Thomas

The Flow—

1. Find people to read the two scriptures and one person to light the candle.
2. Do a drama in first person as a woman at the empty tomb.
3. Read 1 Peter 1:3–9
4. Play "The Hallelujah Chorus" while showing PowerPoint slides alternating God's creation in nature and humanity's places of worship.
5. Share some Easter reflections and stories with one another.

PENTECOST—BORN OF SPIRIT—DOING THE PRACTICAL LABOR
EARLY JUNE TO LATE NOVEMBER

Music—"Happy Birthday"—Be ready to sing it together.
Visuals—Festive balloons and birthday party decorations. Red background, heart and dove banner. Birthday cake. Opening scene video of feather on the wind from movie *Forrest Gump.* Posterboard of the world.

Scripture—

Acts 2:1–21	Account of Pentecost
1 Corinthians 12:3–13	Different gifts, one body
Romans 12:1–8	Offer ourselves and our gifts to the One who made us.

The Flow—

1. Ask three people to read scripture, one to light the candles on the birthday cake, one to blow them out, and one to cut and serve the cake.
2. Read Acts 2:1–21.
3. Sing Happy Birthday to the Church, blow out the candles, and share the cake.
4. View the excerpt from *Forrest Gump* and have a discussion about the Holy Spirit.
5. Read 1 Corinthians 12:3–13.
6. Read Romans 12:2–8.
7. Find magazine and newspaper words or pictures that illustrate people in ministry around the world, doing God's work through Jesus Christ. Paste them on the big, world posterboard.

Additional Resources

Bostrom, Kathleen Long. *For Everything, A Season: A Study of the Liturgical Calendar*, 2005–2006 Horizons Bible Study, Volume. 18, Number 3. (Louisville, KY: Horizons, 2005).

Calhoun, Adele Ahlberg. *Spiritual Disciplines Handbook: Practices That Transform Us, Revised and Expanded.* (Downers Grove, IL: InterVarsity Press, 2005).

Gafke, Arthur. *Pray the Seasons: Pastoral Prayers for Seasons of the Year and of Life.* (Las Vegas, NV: AFG Weavings, 2012).

Gross, Bobby. *Living the Christian Year: Time to Inhabit the Story of God.* (Downers Grove, IL: IVP Books, 2009).

Halverson, Delia. *Teaching & Celebrating the Christian Seasons: A Guide for Pastors, Teachers, and Worship Leaders.* (Nashville, TN: Chalice Press, 2002).

Ireton, Kimberlee Conway. *The Circle of Seasons: Meeting God in the Church Year.* (Downers Grove, IL: IVP Books, 2008).

Lavigne, Michaele. *Living the Way of Jesus: Practicing the Christian Calendar One Week at a Time.* (Kansas City, MO: The Foundry Publishing, 2019).

Nouwen, Henri J.M. Michael Ford, ed. *Eternal Seasons: A Spiritual Journey Through the Church's Year.* (Notre Dame, IN: Ave Maria Press, 2004, 2007).

Stookey, Laurence Hall. *Calendar: Christ's Time for the Church.* (Nashville, TN: Abingdon, 1996).

Webber, Robert E. *Ancient-Future Time: Forming Spirituality Through the Christian Year.* (Grand Rapids, MI: Baker Publishing Group, 2004).

Acknowledgements

A special Thank You goes to four people who have gone beyond expectations in their expertise, support, and dedication to this project.

Frank J. Nissen has provided the amazing drawings for every chapter of this book, working from the tone and themes for each worship season. He has also given artistic guidance throughout the enterprise, and generous collaboration on the cover, text, and visuals from first page to last.

Carol S. Kern has given both inspiration and the content of her "Worship Arts Through the Christian Year" workshop in this Expanded Edition. Her design and teaching of this workshop models the kind of interactive, structured experience that excellent learning is meant to be. It has been an honor to work alongside her.

Rebecca Inch-Partridge has served as my editor, author manager, and mentor from the manuscript stage to the final production and launching of this Expanded Edition as well as the original book. Her experience, support, persistence, and follow-through have made this book possible.

John Reinhardt has demonstrated a lifetime of skill and generosity of spirit as the formatter of both the original and this Expanded Edition of *Tossed in Time*. His book building experience as John Reinhardt Book Design has produced more than three thousand books thus far, making a world of difference to thousands of readers.

My thanks also goes to members and friends in the **Gold Country Writers**, whose critiques, questions, and suggestions have improved wording and honed this book's focus over these years.

The wave photo on the cover comes from the personal generosity of **Mario Caruso** at Unsplash.com. The cover was produced by **Advantage Marketing and Printing**, Auburn, California in a spirit of teamwork and good will.

About the Author, Illustrator, and Workshop Leader

REV. DR. BETSY SCHWARZENTRAUB, AUTHOR
Worship is the heartbeat of God's people. Betsy Schwarzentraub seeks to strengthen our experience of it in her role as an author, publisher, speaker, and preacher. An ordained minister in The United Methodist Church since the 1970s, she has pastored multiple congregations, was a nationwide consultant in holistic stewardship, and has served as Director of Stewardship for her denomination and in California-Nevada.

Betsy is a member of the Fellowship of Worship Artists, and of the Fellowship of Spiritual Directors and Retreat Leaders, known as "Hearts on Fire." Particularly in these post-COVID days, she has encouraged healing, new beginnings, and finding a new rhythm through the worship seasons. Find her Author Page on Facebook at https://www.facebook.com/BetsySchwarzentraubAuthor.

FRANK J. NISSEN, ILLUSTRATOR AND ARTISTIC DIRECTOR
Frank Nissen grew up in the heart of the Gold Country. He developed early interests in drawing and writing. He graduated from the Art Center College of Design in Pasadena, California. After serving in the Army, he worked in the animation field for forty years, doing visual and story development. He still loves to draw and does it often.

However, writing now consumes most of Frank's energy. He is the author of *Fortune's Call: A Gold Rush Odyssey*. It is Book One of a forthcoming trilogy.

Carol S. Kern, designer and teacher of Worship Arts workshop

Carol Kern is a church musician and visual artist. She has consulted and led workshops in Worship and the Arts for decades in church and public school settings. She has been a Director of Music in churches and has established and led music groups for adults and children of all ages.

Carol is a member of the Fellowship of Worship Artists. She was the Western Jurisdiction representative to their national association for four years. For another four years she served as a member of the Worship Task Force for the California-Nevada Annual Conference of The United Methodist Church. She also designed and taught the "Worship Arts" workshop, cited in this book, as part of the California-Nevada Conference Lay Ministers training for local church lay leaders.

Made in the USA
Monee, IL
19 January 2024

51277244R00092